ENCOUNTER AT BENTWATERS

•   •   •

They were staring at a large pyramid-shaped object with a red light on top. It was clearly a machine of some sort, Airman Warren thought, but he had never seen its like before. If he looked at it directly, it seemed that its shape was changing. A ball of light emerged from behind the object. The light separated into three distinct orbs, each containing one creature inside.

The creatures inside the orbs were small, about four feet tall and dressed in what looked like silvery one-piece flight suits. They had overly large black eyes that were dominant features in their faces. The orbs hung in the air in front of the officers until Wing Commander Williams stepped up to them.

To Warren, the creatures seemed to be communicating with Gordon Williams. . . .

•   •   •

UNSOLVED UFO MYSTERIES

THE WORLD'S MOST COMPELLING CASES
OF ALIEN ENCOUNTER

WILLIAM J. BIRNES
AND HAROLD BURT

ASPECT®

WARNER BOOKS

A Time Warner Company

WARNER BOOKS EDITION

Copyright © 2000 by William J. Birnes and Harold Burt

Cover design by Jesse Sanchez / Don Puckey
Cover photo © James Porto / FPG International LLC
Book design by Charles Sutherland

Warner Books, Inc.
1271 Avenue of the Americas
New York, NY 10020

Visit our Web site at
www.twbookmark.com

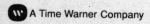 A Time Warner Company

Printed in the United States of America

First Printing: July 2000

10 9 8 7 6 5 4 3 2

ACKNOWLEDGMENTS

The authors wish to thank the editors and writers at *UFO Magazine,* and especially editor in chief Vicki Ecker and news director Don Ecker. Thanks to CAUS director Peter Gersten for allowing us to cite material from his personal contacts page at www.CAUS.org. Thanks also to Dr. Roger Leir, Bill Hamilton of Skywatch, Pam Hamilton, Nikolay Subbotin at RUFORS, Clifford Stone, Peter Robbins, and to all our friends at Orange County and Ventura County MUFON. A special thanks to our research editor, Ron Press, for his almost magical abilities to find information on the Internet that nobody knew existed. We acknowledge also the editorial expertise, insight, but mostly the support of our editor at Warner Books, Betsy Mitchell, editor in chief of Aspect.

Finally, we dedicate this book to our wives, Gina Burt and Nancy Hayfield Birnes, with thanks and love.

> *So womanly, so benigne, and so meke*
> *That in this world, thogh that men wolde seke,*
> *Half hire beaute shulde ment fynde*
> *In creature that formed ys by kynde.*
> *And therefore may I seyn, as thynketh me,*
> *This song in preysyng of this lady fre.*
>
> *Geoffrey Chaucer*

CONTENTS

UNSOLVED UFO
MYSTERIES

CHAPTER 1

What Was Behind the Phoenix Lights?

"If we were being attacked by space aliens we wouldn't be playing these kinds of games."

President Bill Clinton, in response to learning about House of Representatives budget cuts, October 1999

ARIZONA HAS HAD A LONG HISTORY OF REPORTED UFO sightings. For fifty years residents of the state have reported the sightings of strange craft. But in March 1997 there began a series of events that would stun American television audiences from coast to coast, gluing them to evening news broadcasts of strange lights floating through the skies above Phoenix. This event, which continued off and on for the next few months, is known as the Phoenix Lights: formations of yellow, orange, amber, and white lights that flew over the city and surrounding areas along a corridor stretching northwest to southeast.

The well-photographed and videotaped Phoenix Lights were the subject of heavy news coverage, but their origin has never been fully explained. To many investigators, they were UFOs, plain and simple. To oth-

1

ers, they were flares dropped from military aircraft as part of an exercise.

The Witness Reports

Although March 13, 1997, has been cited as the first appearance of the Phoenix Lights, according to some of the postings on the Internet and phone calls to UFO researchers in the Phoenix area there were sightings of V-shaped configurations of lights even before that date, north and west of Phoenix. One observer was a private pilot who was driving well west of Phoenix along a route that took him near the landing approach paths to Luke Air Force Base. At first he thought the lights ahead of him along the road were landing lights, maybe on a jet coming just a bit too low on its approach to the runway about thirty to forty miles away from him.

This was a kind of yellow light he'd never seen before, and he looked around to see if there were any other strange lights in the sky. He found one, brighter than the first but the same color. When he turned back to check on the position of the original light, it had disappeared.

Just three days later, other families witnessed and photographed strange lights floating over the general vicinity where the yellow lights had been spotted. Each witness knew nothing about the experiences of the others, but the lights continued to appear during the ensuing nights with enough frequency that witnesses began posting their sightings on Internet news groups and Web sites.

Then, on March 13, the light show began in earnest. The first display took place somewhere around 8:30 P.M.

when a series of yellowish orange lights just seemed to turn on in the sky north and west of Phoenix. The first observers didn't report seeing a craft of any kind, simply lights that appeared to float in the air in a straight line, angled back from each other as if they were in a formation. The news media reported at least two separate displays of floating lights that night, one beginning about two hours after sundown and the other two-and-a-half hours after the first. They continued until midnight or even later as the lights traveled across the state of Arizona from the northwest to the southeast.

Some cases of the sightings weren't disclosed until one or two days later when observers called their local newspapers to tell their stories. Gradually, the entire time sequence of the appearance of the lights began to take shape. One report, for example, received at Peter Davenport's National UFO Reporting Center in Seattle, said that a formation of yellow lights appeared in Nevada near Nellis Air Force Base at 8:15, heading south and west. Another sighting, of a flying V of yellow lights, took place near Lake Mead at 7:30 P.M. and appeared to be heading west toward Phoenix. Additionally, two different observers reported seeing a large triangular-shaped arrangement of five yellow lights near Prescott, Arizona, heading west.

Then, it seemed, lights turned up all over the skies over Prescott, Arizona. From 8:15 to 8:30, yellowish orange and yellowish white lights turned on one by one in a V-shaped formation and floated through the skies without a sound. Some of the light formations moved as slowly as fifty miles per hour. Others seemed to move faster and performed sharp turns and other maneuvers.

Courtesy Bill Hamilton.

A computer-generated image of a Phoenix Lights boomerang-shaped craft.

But all the observers reported seeing lights with a similar yellow hue, and most of the lights were flying in either a V or triangle formation. Yet another observer in Prescott reported a cluster of V-shapes, almost like a military chevron of three rows of five yellow-white lights floating overhead without a sound and heading south and west.

There were hundreds of reports of lights over Phoenix, Prescott, and Scottsdale that night. Many of the witnesses said that the lights defined the shape of an object, either a large triangle or a huge V, which blocked the light from the stars overhead. Those witnesses directly beneath the flying object—the UFO for want of a better term—said that not only did it have a well-defined shape, but it covered an area measured by three or more entire city blocks. One person called it the size of a football field, another observer said that it was so large you could land a plane on its surface, and a third said that it moved like a blimp but had the shape of a huge wedge that blocked out the starlight for over a half mile.

Other eyewitnesses reported anomalies within the configuration of the lights, suggesting that the wedge or triangular formations were just that, formations. One witness who was driving through the city of Glendale with his family reported that he spotted a formation of lights in the shape of a triangle flying slowly a few thousand feet above them. The witness watched as one of the lights from the trailing edge of the triangle separated from the formation and moved to a light in the leading edge. Whatever this particular configuration of lights was, the lights didn't behave as though they were running lights fixed to a large aircraft, but rather as though they were separate navigable aircraft attached to a larger platform.

Another witness in Scottsdale observed similar movement. In this case, a triangular formation of lights headed south over the city at 8:30, then returned about ninety minutes later and seemed to launch individual spheres of yellow light from its formation that realigned themselves into a mile-wide arc. The object then disappeared.

One young child who had gone to bed by 8:00 that evening reported seeing a beam of bright light from the outside travel along her bedroom wall. The child's description of the time and direction of the beam of light correspond with reports from neighbors who witnessed a large, bright formation of lights that floated at a low altitude above their houses and cast a beam of light along the houses as it passed by. The witnesses' drawings of the shape of the object defined by the lights showed that they had seen a large flying triangle similar to the objects seen by hundreds of others that same night.

The closer witnesses were to the flying lights, the more detailed the descriptions they gave. One couple said they could make out gray panels on the underside of the triangle as it floated over their house, and that one of the light spheres from the leading edge of the triangle detached, floated away from the triangle, and then returned. It looked to them like a docking maneuver, all of it accomplished without the sound of jet engines, propellers, or rotors of any kind. They said they couldn't even hear the sound of rushing air as the triangle passed by into the night.

Observers were impressed by the huge size of the triangles, particularly when the triangles were flying low and passed over landmarks that allowed the witnesses to estimate wingspan and length. One witness, in a car driving along a freeway west of Phoenix, was able to get a good look. She described a metallic structure forming the underside of a triangle, flying southeast, and what looked like panels surrounded by spherical lights along the edges. She was also able to make out the object's wingspan, claiming that it reached across the freeway and was well over a mile wide.

Two other witnesses also used ground landmarks to determine the size of the flying triangle they saw floating over a newly developed real estate subdivision.

Knowing the layout of the subdivision and the distances between the streets, these witnesses reported the object's wingspan had to have been well over a mile and probably closer to two. Hours after these observers returned home they saw the object again, at which point a flight of military jets tried to intercept it, but failed to catch it when it shot up vertically.

Other witness reports vary, but all of them seem too astounding to be true. In one case a witness reported that he watched a commercial aircraft almost collide with a large triangle. Why, as the aircraft lights approached the floating lights on the triangle, didn't the aircraft pilot pick up the object on radar, and why didn't the collision warning system activate? Why didn't the control tower vector the aircraft away? Surely civilian flight control radar must have returned a collision alert between the two objects. Instead, the aircraft simply passed above the triangle as if it weren't there. This suggests that the triangle did not appear as a signature on any of the radar screens. To the pilot as well as to flight controllers in the tower, the triangle wasn't really there at all.

For another observer on a terrace, the seemingly rigid metallic structure that held the lights in place seemed to disappear when the object floated past the moon. Instead of obliterating the moon, the object became translucent and the moon shone yellow at the edges of the triangle just as if the object were not a solid piece of metal at all. After the object had passed across the surface of the moon, its metallic shape seemed to return and the object headed along its way, leaving stunned witnesses on neighboring terraces in its wake. It was a spectacle none of them had ever seen before.

Still another witness, who viewed an object that floated a hundred feet above his house, reported to a newspaper that the object was the largest flying structure he had ever seen. As the object passed overhead, the witness thought he saw one of the lights split into two and change color before it returned to the wedge structure of the formation. The object moved very slowly as it floated noiselessly over Phoenix and finally disappeared behind a mountain range. As observations continued through the night, investigators who track UFO reports began to correlate the direction, speed, and configurations of the lights to determine whether the sightings were simply random or if they defined a course. Laid out across a map grid, the formations seemed to be moving from the northwestern part of Arizona, over Phoenix and its surrounding areas through valleys bordered north and south by mountain ranges, to the south and east of Phoenix and then back again along a well-defined air corridor.

Hundreds of witnesses were struck by a sense of awe and amazement at the level of technology they'd observed. Living in such close proximity to airports and military bases, many of these observers were familiar with the outlines of military aircraft, even the huge air force cargo planes that landed at Luke Air Force Base, and were able to recognize that the shape of these triangles and wedges was very different from the military and commercial planes that were usually in the skies. The very unfamiliarity of these triangles and wedges, whether or not they were extraterrestrial in origin, made them unidentified flying objects.

The Public Reaction

Public frenzy over the Phoenix Lights was fueled by the sheer number of witnesses who reported the phenomena. Unlike a sighting made by two or three people and reported to a skeptical and disbelieving public, the Phoenix sightings took place over entire neighborhoods in which friends and relatives reported seeing the same things at the same time. Neighbors called neighbors who corroborated one another's sightings. Then there was the videotape evidence which, despite disagreement among experts as to the nature of what was photographed, nevertheless conveyed visually to television viewers across the country the sheer fascination of the light spectacle and the unearthly awe people experienced when they saw it.

Witnesses and private citizens, as well as radio stations and newspapers who'd taken calls from observers, demanded explanations for the mysterious lights from the U.S. Air Force, local police and fire departments, the governor, and even the local Phoenix city council. But in the face of air force denials that anything out of the ordinary had taken place on the night of March 13, other agencies were at a loss to offer any explanations, even though sheriff's officers and fire departments tried to follow up after the onslaught of phone calls from frantic witnesses demanding to know what was happening.

By the next day, the story about the lights and copies of videotapes were circulating throughout the Phoenix area. Local news television stations were already sending teams and camera vans out to interview witnesses, review the videos they'd shot, and put together segments for that evening's news broadcasts. The competition for original stories had gotten intense because the images of the floating lights were so incredibly dramatic. This was the age of the home video camera, a device that had become as commonplace in households as the old Kodak box cameras had been in the 1950s. Accordingly, witnesses told news crews, when they saw something that didn't look like a plane, they aimed their cameras and shot. The collective result was hundreds of hours of video that captured one night of almost Twilight Zone eeriness in the skies over Phoenix.

Hardened news editors realized that this was not simply another wacky UFO sighting but something real, something that had been witnessed by thousands of people that had driven them to call 911 en masse. The news organizations joined the onslaught of calls to military authorities, demanding some sort of explanation for the lights even if only a routine confirmation or denial that there had been objects in the sky on the night of March 13. They also joined the callers to the fire department and the sheriff to see what the nature of the 911 calls were, whether there were tape recordings available of the calls, and what the public safety authorities did to respond.

The Official Response

The day after the sighting reports, the air force announced that it could report no out-of-the-ordinary radar contacts on the night of March 13, certainly not the kinds of contacts that would have corresponded to the hundreds of sightings over Phoenix and its neighboring cities. Moreover, the air force public information representative at Luke Air Force Base announced that all of their planes had been secured for the night, indirectly denying that Luke had scrambled any fighters to investigate the reported formations. Witnesses who had seen jets trying to close with the lights were incredulous: the air force was denying what observers said they had seen with their own eyes.

Civilian flight control authorities at the Phoenix airport gave exactly the same response: no radar contacts out of the ordinary, no contacts that would have corresponded with the reported sightings. Commercial aircraft that were in the area reported no collision alerts from radar targets in the area. If you went by what the radar said, it was as if nothing had happened at all. Was it all a mass illusion?

Not at all, a spokesperson for the Maryland Air National Guard finally confirmed a few months later in July after a story broke in *USA Today* and on television that the Maryland Air National Guard, in an operation called Snowbird, had dropped flares in the Phoenix area on the night of March 13. The spokesperson revealed that on the night in question units from the Air National Guard, flying out of Davis-Monthan Air Force Base in Tucson, had dropped high-intensity flares in military training exercises they were conducting in A-10s over the Barry Goldwater Gunnery Test Range fifty miles southwest of Phoenix. The Maryland Air National Guard used the Goldwater range because weather conditions in the southwestern United States were typically far better than those in the Northeast during winter. The original story explained that the flares were dropped in an exercise designed to train pilots on how to deploy flares to draw away incoming heat-seeking surface-to-air missiles. These very bright flares were dropped in formation, the spokesperson said, and, suspended by tiny parachutes invisible in the nighttime sky, would surely account for the anomalous lights observers reported.

In other words, this was exactly the kind of device that would have provided a light show to anyone looking outside that night without returning a radar signature to flight controllers at the local airports or to the radars at Luke Air Force Base. Except there was one problem, people living near the Goldwater range didn't report seeing flares over the range at the time the Air National Guard said they were in the air. However, the flare explanation did comport with the explanation from Luke Air Force Base that none of *its* fighter planes were in the air that night. They had been Maryland Air National planes conducting their own military exercises over the Barry Goldwater Test Range. But because they had been flying out of Davis-Monthan and not out of Luke AFB, the public affairs officer at Luke said she had no knowledge of the flight schedules at Davis-Monthan until after the Maryland Air National Guard flare story broke. At that point, she said, she checked with her counterpart at Davis-Monthan and confirmed that although her original story that no flare-dropping exercises had been conducted at Luke was a correct report, she did not know at the time that another air force base had hosted an out-of-state Air National Guard unit that was flying over the Goldwater range at the time of the Phoenix Lights reports.

The intensity of the phone calls to media and the offices of public safety continued even after the Maryland

Air National Guard announcement in July. The amount of media coverage the lights generated could not be completely ignored, while at the same time, UFO researchers such as Bill Hamilton of Skywatch, who has written his own book on the Phoenix Lights, disputed the Air National Guard's explanation of the flare story. Hamilton pointed out, first, that the schedules were incompatible. People were seeing lights in the sky both before and after the Maryland Air National Guard took off from Davis-Monthan. Then, Hamilton argued, the Air National Guard itself had changed its own story. First it said that the exercise was designed to train pilots when to deploy the flares as countermeasures to the missiles. However, after witnesses to the Phoenix Lights said that the formations were too high in the sky to have been low-altitude antiaircraft countermeasures, the Maryland Air National Guard changed its story, now saying that the flares were really higher-altitude illumination devices. But, as Hamilton pointed out, what could they illuminate at 15,000 feet except for clouds? And what about the reports that some of the hanging lights seemed to fly in straight lines or even gain altitude? Could these have been optical illusions?

Hamilton had an additional problem with the air force explanation, which, he says, still hasn't been resolved. Because Luke Air Force Base controls the Goldwater test range, it should have been fully aware that there was a training exercise there that night even if the planes flew in from Davis-Monthan. Why didn't Luke report it right away instead of waiting until July to comment on the reports in the media about flares. In other words, the Maryland Air National Guard's story made no sense.

Adding to the media fervor, the lights were still continuing to appear in many locations around Phoenix, Arizona, returning on successive nights, even while the original Lights story was being debated in the news. People were complaining. They had seen something, and there was videotape already playing on local and statewide television that clearly showed some kind of light formations in the sky.

In Phoenix, city council member Frances Barwood tried to get the council to demand answers from the air force. Other council members refused to go along with her request, and she quickly became an object of derision, especially from the mayor of Phoenix, as well as others who were nervous about being associated with any politician publicly seeking information about UFOs. When Frances Barwood's term on the city council ended, she ran for Arizona Secretary of State but was defeated, despite grassroots support from the UFO community.

With demands for some kind of official response growing among the public, then Arizona governor Fyfe Symington called a news conference near the end of August 1997 at which he promised the media he would authorize a special investigator. People seemed stunned at the news. Only once before in recent memory had an elected official demanded an investigation of a UFO report. That had been late member of the House of Representatives Steve Schiff from New Mexico. In 1995 he asked the government to account for the 1947 crash at Roswell, which resulted in the government's revealing that the aircraft that was retrieved was a top secret radar balloon. Now, a state governor was demanding an investigation. And this time, the UFOs being investigated had been seen by not just a few people, but many hundreds. But within days of the announcement, Governor Symington called a second press conference at which he announced he would reveal to the audience the culprit behind the Phoenix Lights sightings. Then a person wearing a little-green-man alien costume walked to the podium. The note-taking reporters dissolved into guffaws as the governor dismissed the entire event as mass hallucinations and hysteria.

For those people who believed they'd been witness to a real UFO event, and for many others who claimed some sort of contact with alien beings either through abduction or previous sightings, Governor Symington's news conference was an insult. So what if the governor didn't believe the Phoenix Lights were out of the ordinary? many observers said. It wasn't an excuse to poke fun at individuals who claimed they'd been victims of a traumatic experience.

The news conference, if it had been an attempt to throw cold water on the rumors of a UFO invasion, actually served the opposite purpose. Observers were now more convinced than ever that there was some kind of official cover-up going on. Witnesses were put off by the air force denials, the apparent inability of local government to come up with an explanation, and now the deliberate attempt to make fun of the event. What was going on?

The Media Response

The national broadcast media had already been running video of the Phoenix Lights when the Symington news conference provided them with even more fuel for the fire. Within days, both the tabloid media and news magazine shows were carrying Phoenix Lights video, while radio talk shows interviewed witnesses and investigators from the UFO community. Now, for the first time, live witness statements accompanied the eerie videos, and stories of the shapes and sizes of objects began to emerge.

It wasn't just the lights, witnesses told national audiences as they showed off their balconies and terraces to reporters, it was the configurations of the lights and what you could see inside that got them so excited. There were shapes—real, definable shapes—that blotted out the sky and captured reflections from the city lights below. And it wasn't until television audiences actually saw the places where the videos originated that a lot of the stories began to make sense. Many witnesses had stood on balconies and terraces built into the hillsides. Therefore, people weren't just looking up at a series of lights, some of them were on a direct level or close enough to the floating objects to see the details they had described. Others said they could almost look *down* on the objects because the objects had been flying so low. The national news coverage and the appearances of these witnesses on news shows suddenly gave the Phoenix Lights a whole new perspective.

The Researchers

In the aftermath of the Phoenix Lights sightings professional engineers, Ufologists, skeptics, and debunkers all presented their analyses of what people had seen in the skies. The announcement from the Maryland Air National Guard provided the most straightforward explanation and certainly the easiest to understand. Formations of flares might easily be confused with some sort of craft in a nighttime sky. Because they were moving forward at the same time they were slowly dropping, they could easily give the impression that they were actually flying very slowly on a level course without a sound. And maybe, depending upon the angle, they might even seem to be rising. But the flare story still doesn't explain how high-intensity illumination devices dropped fifty miles away from Phoenix could be seen floating directly over rooftops and balconies.

Airplanes and helicopters, even if they were flying at high altitudes—which these lights certainly were not—would not fly silently. There would be some noise from the engines. And because almost all of the observers reported noiseless lights, A-10s, helicopters, or other conventional military aircraft can probably be ruled out. It's not impossible that the army was flying formations of black helicopters with silent rotors or that the air force could have been testing its neutral buoyancy aircraft, huge triangular-shaped transport aircraft that have been in development for years. These large and stealthy transport planes are capable of moving very slowly and might well be almost invisible to radar. This might account for the lack of radar contact that night—assuming that the air force was telling the truth when it announced that nothing had turned up on radar over Luke Air Force Base. If, however, observers were accurate in their descriptions of spherical lights that detached from the formation and moved about independently, it would mean that they might have seen something else.

Some analysts have speculated that because there were different configurations of lights on March 13 and on ensuing days, it's also possible that different observers reported different phenomena. Some people might have seen flares while other people might have seen test flights of air force super lifters whose presence, like the test flights of the stealth F-117 and the B-2, were classified under national security for at least a decade and therefore never announced, confirmed, or even acknowledged by a denial. Therefore, if there were air force test flights that night as well as a military flare-dropping exercise, between the flares and the test flights, successive arrays of lights and huge black triangular shapes that floated over Phoenix might just be explained.

Or maybe not.

Flares

The flare theory has at least four problems, according to Bill Hamilton and other UFO analysts. First, and probably the easiest to reconcile, is the time differential between the sightings of lights and reported time of the flare drops. The Maryland Air National Guard announced they began their flare drops after nine in the evening, yet the earliest flare sightings took place shortly after eight. So if flares are the explanation for the Phoenix Lights, how can we account for at least a one-hour discrepancy between the reported beginning of the military exercise and the reports of the first formations of lights? There are also discrepancies between the location of the test range where the flares were dropped and the observers who reported the sightings of lights shortly after eight. But these are less troublesome than the question over the different times.

The easiest answer is that the reported times could be less than accurate, that somebody is making a mistake. If some of the flares were dropped early and not all the observers were careful about the times they gave for their sightings, it's conceivable that at least some of the Phoenix Lights sights were flares. It's also conceivable that some witnesses became disoriented with respect to times, directions, and geographical locations and actually were looking at flares in one direction when they thought they were looking at something else in another direction.

The second issue is the discrepancy between reports of colored lights and bright white high-intensity flares. Analysts who reviewed the Maryland Air National Guard's reports determined that the special flares they dropped would burn bright white and give off heat. In particular, these flares can serve as decoys for enemy surface-to-air missiles such as the ones deployed by Serb forces in the recent Bosnian and Kosovo air campaigns. When deployed by allied aircraft, the flare, suspended by its small parachute, slowly descends, drawing off enemy missiles that might be looking for a heat signature.

However, the lights observed by most of the witnesses were not the bright white of antiaircraft countermeasures flares but instead, depending upon who was describing them, were of amber, yellow, or even reddish orange. Therefore, even if we can account for a discrepancy in time and geographical location, the difference in color indicates that at least some of the observers were not looking at high-intensity flares no matter what atmospheric conditions were present that could have somewhat altered the observable color.

UFO analysts also cite sighting reports from witnesses who not only say they've watched previous flare drops over the test ranges in the area, but also have had military experience and know what flares look like. Many of these witnesses reported in interviews that what they saw were not flares by any means.

Flight trajectory was another one of the key factors UFO analysts used in determining whether the objects of March 13, 1997, were flares or self-propelled objects. An object that simply floats to the ground even as it moves forward has one flight signature, while an object that seems to move and navigate under its own power has quite another, UFO analysts have argued. This, the third criterion in determining the difference between flares and the Phoenix Lights, was critical to most of the witnesses because they report that the objects didn't just float to the ground, but that they flew on a level path, seemed to turn in unison as if they were attached to a larger object, accelerated, and even turned to a new heading. And if they were flares deployed over test ranges fifty miles away, why did they seem to hover, only a hundred or so feet directly above rooftops and terraces in the city of Phoenix, giving witnesses an astonishingly close look at objects they called "shapes" rather than flares?

Other experts argued that the floating lights people claimed to have seen were only an optical illusion, a combination of the intensity of the flares, the forward momentum of the formation, and the retinal memory of the bright image against the darkness of the night. The result was a sense that the objects were somehow flying when in fact they were only gently falling, while their momentum at the speed of the A-10s that dropped them carried them forward.

Ufologists claim, however, that the lights moved forward together as if they were connected, while flares, even the most sophisticated flares, would act independently of one another. Separate objects still have to obey the laws of random motion even when they are launched at exactly the same time and in the same direction. At some point, microcurrents of air, variations in the way the separate parachutes behave, up- and downdrafts, and even the small time differential between the launches will cause the flares to exhibit aerodynamic qualities. They might descend at different rates, change direction with respect to one another, and go in different directions in their respective trajectories. These lights, witnesses say, did none of that. In those cases when it seemed as if they were fixed along the leading or trailing edges of a giant triangle, the lights stayed in the same place, were unwavering in their intensity, and did not descend at different rates.

Perhaps the most bizarre of all the sightings of the Phoenix Lights were those of spheres that seemed to separate from the formation and fly to another light, or break off completely from the rest of the group, and then return. While lights that fly in different directions might look like flares, some critics have commented, the lights that seemed to regroup with the formation or fly next to another sphere and then return to the formation behaved just like independently piloted or controlled aircraft.

UFO histories contain many reports of flying orbs or spheres over the desert states since the 1940s. Green orbs, in particular, were a common enigma during the 1950s and '60s. However, seeing these orbs as part of larger formations or even attached to larger craft would be something relatively new.

What about the large triangular shapes that seemed to drift at low altitudes through the canyon passes and over the rooftops at ridiculously low speeds? Were there any conventional explanations that could account for the triangles or flying wing shapes? If it weren't for the huge size—particularly the estimates of a one-and-a-half- to two-mile wingspan—some ufologists believe that Lockheed's neutral buoyancy triangular transport planes could account for the triangular shapes that witnesses saw that night. The black stealth transports are designed not to return a radar signature and to move at slow speeds, kept aloft, like blimps, by a buoyancy system that allows them to float. If the overwhelming size of the transports confused witnesses, especially in the darkness, to estimate inaccurately the ground landmarks from wingtip to wingtip, the possibility exists that the reported two-mile wingspan could actually be much less. If that's the case, then maybe the flying triangles witnesses saw were the same aircraft that have been described in aviation and science magazines and have been observed over California and other places in the United States, classified aircraft in the final phases of testing before being announced to the public (for much more on flying triangles, see Chapter 2).

The CAUS Lawsuit

Whether some of the Phoenix Lights were flares or flying triangles, the response of the State of Arizona, the U.S. Air Force, and the Department of Defense has been silence. Even where witnesses steadfastly repeated that the lights they saw, because of their colors, their flight patterns, and their ability to climb and navigate, could not possibly have been flares, the U.S. government still refused to admit that there was anything out of the ordinary in the skies over Phoenix. Finally, in 1999, Arizona attorney Peter Gersten, the head of an organization called Citizens Against UFO Secrecy and a columnist for *UFO Magazine,* filed suit against the United States, seeking relief in federal court against what he termed an "incursion of unidentified and unusual aerial craft" and, on behalf of the citizens of the State of Arizona, an end to "unlawful violations of their civil, legal and constitutional rights by non-human entities."

The lawsuit asserts that after Gersten's repeated attempts to seek information from the State of Arizona and the Department of Defense about the nature of the Phoenix Lights, and receiving no response, CAUS is seeking remedy from the federal government which, under Article IV of the Constitution, is required to protect the individual states and the citizens thereof against invasion. Gersten specifies that just such an invasion is being carried out by "entities, non-human in appearance, who have unlawfully entered each of the United States, including the State of Arizona, and remain unlawfully within Arizona, committing acts that if done by humans would be prosecutable under Arizona and federal law."

By suing United States Attorney General Janet Reno, Secretary of Defense William Cohen, and Governor of Arizona Jane Hull, CAUS asks the court to require the United States to formulate a plan to investigate, study, identify, and protect the residents of Arizona against this invasion and to maintain jurisdiction over the case and monitor the plan to protect American citizens from an alien invasion.

In letters to Governor Hull, Attorney General Reno, and the Secretary of Defense, Peter Gersten described the nature of what he called "an ongoing invasion which is continually being ignored by government officials due to its strangeness and thus continues unimpeded." Writing on behalf of those who signed affidavits for CAUS, Gersten asserts: "These residents describe an invasion that is 'silent' due to its nature, but an invasion nonetheless. Simply stated, it takes the form of continuous incursions in the skies over your state by aerial 'craft' which pose a threat simply by their ability to perform beyond present day technology. Also present as part of this silent invasion are nonconsensual trespasses, assaults, false imprisonment, rapes, and kidnappings by allegedly non-human perpetrators. These acts constitute crimes under both state and federal law, yet there has not been one major investigation by your Agency. The fact that the perpetrators have been continually described as non-human in appearance unfortunately has negated both the seriousness of the allegations and the believability of the eyewitnesses. This is a travesty and injustice, especially since these acts have been occurring for over thirty years and have been reported by thousands of people throughout the United States. Affidavits are available from your residents swearing to these facts and circumstances."

The letters go on to describe the craft as "unidentified, unknown, and technologically advanced craft infringing the skies of this State. These craft take the form of triangular, 'v,' or delta shaped aerial objects." The lawsuit cites letters Gersten has received from citizens of Arizona in which they told stories of floating colored lights, flying triangles, and appearances of strange craft that dated back to the 1980s and continued well past the March 13, 1997, date of the initial flyovers of the Phoenix Lights.

In one description, an Arizona resident tells the story of what she believed was actual communication with a UFO that seemed to follow her along a road known to local residents as "the road to Nowhere."

"Another time we went to the road to Nowhere, we watched three unusual color-changing lights at once. One stationary one to the northwest of us, one over the southern end of the White Tanks to the east of us, and a very active one that danced around in the sky to the south of us. When we got tired around 1:00–1:30 am, I announced loudly that it was time to go home and the light to the east of us blinked out suddenly. We laughed about that and when I looked up again a moment later, it blinked back on. We were getting in our vehicles to leave when it blinked out again and stayed out. We had to drive north a little way to make a U-turn to return to I-10. When we pulled around to the south, we were greeted by an eerie sight. The light we'd been watching to the south (which had been east of the road all evening) had seemingly lined itself up directly in front of us still very low on the horizon so that we drove directly toward it.

When we got on I-10 going east, it paced us all the way back to Goodyear (20 miles or so) and ended up over the Estrellas when we got home.

"We go out there to watch the sky probably three to four times a year, and though we watch a lot of orange lights and ones that blink blue/red/white, these are about the most dramatic sightings we've had out there. My sister, a friend and I had a large blue light over the northern end of the White Tanks that seemed to blink back at us when we blinked a flashlight toward it last year. Next day, we heard from other people that they'd seen the same object. This southwestern corner of the Valley of the Sun does seem to be a 'hotspot' for lights in the sky."

Another Phoenix resident reported "missing time" during a party at his house in 1996 when he and his two friends could not account for almost an hour's passing. When they went outside to try to reorient themselves, they noticed two UFOs hovering just over the horizon. "Two craft were quickly approaching each other, one from the north and the other from the south, and were a greenish white haze shaped like an odd turtle shell. They came within about five miles of each other and began rising together vertically in the sky. At around 30,000 feet they fused together and became one craft and started continuing up again. At 60,000 feet they broke apart and hesitated again before rising some more to about 90,000 feet, all within about a minute or two. Next, they changed direction straight east towards us. They were still about five miles apart again, and one of the silent craft, both of them ten times larger than a 747, was flying directly over the northern boundary of Lake Havasu City and the other over the desert. We were totally quiet during the entire sighting as one flew almost directly overhead. Underneath were three rows of three lights, and one single last pulsating white light. The lights in the rows were translucent colors and shades we had never seen before. The edges of the craft had a sharp cut to them and there was no glowing haze underneath the craft like what we saw from a distance. They continued on towards Phoenix."

Armed with sightings such as these and reports of abductions, Peter Gersten charges that the government steadfastly refuses to offer any explanations or even assurances that the residents of Arizona are not victims of an invasion by nonhuman entities. Worse, he charges, the government refuses to investigate citizen criminal complaints of break-ins, home invasions, and even abductions and torture that fall within the jurisdiction of both the state and federal governments even though "these non-human entities also violate the laws of each of the United States, including the laws of Arizona, by conducting non-consensual physical acts upon said residents in violation of said residents' civil, legal and constitutionally protected rights."

The CAUS lawsuit, which will gradually work its way up the federal judicial ladder through the appeals courts, is only one of a number of attempts to extract from the government, particularly the military, an explanation for the mystery lights, the formations of orbs and spheres, and the silent floating triangles that continue to this day to appear in the skies over Arizona to the astonishment and fascination of the people who see them.

CHAPTER 2

Flying Triangles

"One thing's for sure, I'll never make fun of people who say they've seen unidentified objects in the sky."

President Jimmy Carter

*I*N THE RECENT DEBATES OVER THE EXISTENCE OF EX-traterrestrial UFOs, one of the most consistently talked about sightings are of aircraft called "flying triangles." These objects, which vary in size and shape and have appeared in different parts of the country, have actually been observed since the late 1940s. Over the past twenty years, however, the sightings have become increasingly numerous and more and more people have called various UFO hotlines to describe them. Some have called them "triangles," others "flying wings," and still others "floating boomerangs," "crescents," or "flying diamonds." Many of the descriptions talk about the same kinds of experiences and sensations, thus making them appear repetitious. However, the sheer number of these sightings—literally thousands of encounters over twenty to thirty years—makes this an overwhelming body of testimony. Something is really going on here. This chapter talks about flying triangles and what these aircraft might actually be.

Strange Sights

What were the flying wings that seemed to appear out of the southwestern skies during the late 1940s and early 1950s? Were they the precursors of the floating triangles or flying boomerangs that appeared over the Hudson Valley ten years ago and have been seen hovering over defense installations in Europe as recently as last summer? Are they the same craft that were spotted maneuvering for landings in places like Edwards Air Force Base in California and other bases in Montana and Arizona?

Long regarded as UFOs because of their shape and near silent running, their lack of a conventional radar signature, their ability to hover and turn on a dime, and their incredible size, flying triangles have become a holy grail for UFO researchers who believe they're either the alien spacecraft some people refer to as "mother ships" or an advanced aviation weapon reverse-engineered from UFOs.

Flying triangles appear in UFO reports and UFO literature dating back into the 1970s and '80s and continue right through today. They've been sighted over New York's Hudson Valley, in Pennsylvania, and throughout the southwest. Their awesome size and silent running have inspired fears of large alien craft that can navigate the Earth's atmosphere and seemingly penetrate sophisticated national air defense systems with ease, invisible to the most powerful military tracking and targeting radars. Even in the middle of large metropolitan areas, such as the Greater New York region and along the Southern California coastline, residents have claimed to have seen flying triangles floating overhead. And their descriptions of these craft sound remarkably the same.

Early Sightings

As long ago as the 1930s aircraft designers were testing the aeronautical possibilities of the flying wing, one variation of which was actually built by Curtis Aviation. By the late 1940s the United States military was experimenting with flying wing or delta shapes, some of which might have been based on the jet-powered flying wing developed by German aircraft designers Reimar and Walter Horten for the Luftwaffe late in World War II.

These flying wings or boomerangs, one of which went into production as the YB-49, would have been strange sights in the southwestern skies in the years after World War II. Maybe it was just such a flying wing that a pilot named Kenneth Arnold saw over the Cascade Mountains in Washington in 1947, when he reported a crescent-shaped object whose motion he described to reporters as a "skipping through the air like a saucer" (thus reportedly originating the term "flying saucer"). Maybe it was an experimental flying wing that witnesses saw being pulled out of the desert outside of Roswell in 1947. Or maybe these were really extraterrestrial spacecraft that were making their first appearance and became the model for aircraft that were later developed for the air force.

Besides Kenneth Arnold's flying crescent, the first

known observation of an object referred to as a flying wing or triangle took place in California. The witness, who was sixteen or seventeen years old at the time, reported years later that on one evening in the late 1940s or very early 1950s she was lying on her back on the grass of her family's property in Los Angeles, just gazing at the evening sky, when she saw a dark triangular-shaped object that blocked out the stars. There were lights on the leading edge of the object, and it made no sound as it slowly moved along a steady course across the sky directly over her. She lost sight of it as it moved north and disappeared. The image of a craft in the warm California night stayed with this woman for almost fifty years until she finally made a report of the sighting to Citizens Against UFO Secrecy in 1996.

Almost twenty-five years later, another observer reported seeing a similar triangular or boomerang-shaped object. The sighting took place in the summer of 1974 while the observer was parked at the Ascot Drive-In Movie Theater in Cuyahoga Falls, Ohio. There, a huge, sharply defined, completely black, boomerang-shaped object came into view over the movie screen. It was so gigantic, the witness wasn't able to estimate its size accurately. It seemed to him so close that he could have hit it with a rock as it blotted out the nighttime sky, stars and all. Noiseless and without lights, it traveled in a straight line from the northwest to the southeast, moving so slowly it appeared to be floating like a seabird on invisible currents. People watching the picture stepped out of their cars, pointing in excitement at the real-life show over their heads. Then the motion picture on the screen just stopped.

The drive-in audience behaved in what some researchers have called the "Oz effect," a collective display of bewilderment at an awe-inspiring event which causes a near shutdown of cerebral functions. That's what the witness believed was happening to all of the members of the audience because no one said or did anything except stand there in the darkness and stare at this object as it passed over. Then in an eerie sequence, almost everyone in the audience, moving like automatons, got back into their respective cars, and the movie started up again. No one knew for sure what had stopped the film in the first place, but people suspected it was some kind of energy wave generated by the floating triangle, the same kind of energy that created the Oz effect.

The witness and a few others continued to watch the object until it disappeared over the horizon and they couldn't make out its shape anymore. The entire sighting lasted fifteen to twenty minutes. Mysteriously, and maybe a carryover of the Oz effect, neither the witness nor any of the others who saw the object talked about it among themselves or even asked any questions about what had just happened. It was odd, the witness recalls, because it was almost as if the entire event never took place. In fact, the witness forgot the whole thing until a few years after the event when he was reading a UFO book in which the writer described the same type of occurrence. At that point, the witness's memories of the event at the drive-in flooded back to him. Was this a form of missing time that had affected the entire movie audience?

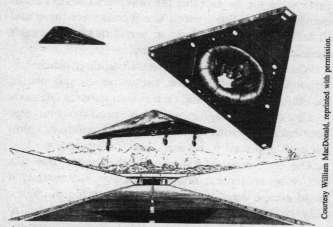

Courtesy William MacDonald, reprinted with permission.

An artist's conception of flying triangle aircraft.

New York and Hudson Valley Sightings

Was it the same craft, a UFO, or the modern U.S. Air Force version of a flying wing that appeared over the Hudson Valley north of New York City during the 1980s and '90s, even flying over the city itself? These craft were observed by hundreds of New Yorkers, in particular those residents on Manhattan's West Side with a view of the Hudson River. One couple who reported the sightings lived on West 23rd Street and 7th Avenue, next to the Chelsea Hotel. During a particularly hot and muggy Fourth of July holiday, the couple, lifelong New Yorkers, noticed 747-sized, stealthlike aircraft flying up and down the Hudson, which was about four avenues to the west of them. The objects seemed like planes at first except for the fact that the observers couldn't make out the edges of the objects. These craft were fuzzy and ill defined, which lent them an unreal quality. The craft made no sound as they floated by.

Watching from the roof of their building, which corresponded to the 18th floor, the witnesses saw one of the craft head uptown and then fifteen minutes later saw another craft, although it could have been the same one, head back downtown. Painted in a dark, military color, the craft appeared to be searching for something.

The craft returned every night that week. Was this part of an air force exercise to test how successfully it could escape detection on radar while flying through a busy air corridor, or was this, as other appearances of these craft might have been, a way to introduce strange craft to the public to test how successful a UFO cover story worked? Whatever it was, the sightings of flying triangles continued unabated, and not only in New York City.

Up and down the Hudson River, from New York Harbor north to Cornwall-on-Hudson and even past Poughkeepsie, people who lived in the Hudson Valley reported flying triangle sightings through the late 1970s and into the '80s. During the middle 1980s, UFO lawyer Peter Gersten has said, there was a near epidemic of sightings that ultimately prompted him to gather a list of prominent UFO researchers at his home in Peekskill for a conference. Out of that meeting grew the Brewster conference on UFO and abduction phenomena, attended by over 1,000 people, many of them area residents who had actually seen the flying triangles floating over their homes. This conference, with speakers such as abduction researcher Budd Hopkins and writer Whitley Streiber, sought to put the flying triangle sightings into the greater context of UFO encounters and the presence of an alien intelligence on planet Earth. One of the first general conferences prompted by flying triangle sightings, it helped create a reporting network which catalogs flying triangle sightings and is available both at Peter Gersten's CAUS Internet Web site and *UFO Magazine*'s Project Blue Book II, also on the Internet.

Sightings in the Desert

A famous radio personality filed a report of flying triangles on the Citizens Against UFO Secrecy Web site a few years after the New York sighting. In August 1994, at approximately 11:30 P.M., after finishing a broadcast from a studio in Las Vegas, he and his wife were driving home under clear skies and a nearly full moon, the only source of light on a very dark night. As they turned onto a narrow road, the witness in the passenger seat noticed a strange movement coming from the left and slightly behind the car. She could see through the rear window a huge, dark object moving toward them and began to yell at her husband, "What the hell is that?"

They stopped and watched a huge, triangle-shaped object float across the rural Nevada valley where they lived from southeast to northwest at about 150 to 200 feet above them and moving more slowly than any aircraft they had ever seen. There was a white, strobing light on the nose of the craft, and two stationary white lights on the rear. And between the lights was a shape big enough to blot out the stars and moon as it passed.

Yet for all its size, the most unnerving part of this sighting for the couple was that there was absolutely no noise as it passed by. As they stood beside the car gaping in wonder at the shape, not a single sound could they hear around them except for crickets chirping unseen in the darkness of the scrub and chaparral. They watched for more than five minutes as the thing drifted across the valley before they lost sight of it over the horizon. If there had been any doubt in the radio commentator's mind about the existence of strange objects in the sky, the sighting of this graceful and mysterious flying triangle went a long way to dispel it.

A year later a man from neighboring Utah filed a report about a very similar object, this time flying in concert with other triangular objects. On the night of June 19, 1995, at 10:30 P.M., he reported to the CAUS online archives of flying triangle sightings; he saw something very strange in the night sky that he'd never seen before or since. He was looking in the northern part of the sky toward 11 o'clock high and saw what he later thought was a "convoy." The first thing he noticed coming toward him were two dark red unblinking lights moving slowly across the sky. Then he saw another two red lights going in the same direction after the first two, one right after the other, each object keeping a steady distance from the others in the sky. Then came what he describes as "a whole bunch" of what he thought were "balls of white lights" flying together but swarming around like fireflies, some twinkling and some not.

"They were not making any kind of noise but were smaller than all the other lights," the witness reported.

He continued, "These lights could not have had wings or they would have bumped each other. Some would kind of go away from others then return into the bunch just as if they were being herded like sheep or something across the sky, going west, exactly toward Area 51 in Nevada, from where I was in Cedar City, Utah. Then in the same 'convoy' there came what looked like one craft with three white lights in a triangular pattern. I could not see a particular craft so I am supposing this craft was triangular in shape, but quite large. Then after that came what I'm sure were two more 'regular' type of airplanes with their sounds and typical lights. Then nothing more. I can only guess that it was some kind of 'escort' of these strange lighted balls being escorted to Area 51."

The government might have had an explanation for the configuration of lights that night in the skies over Utah, but the witness didn't. "I sure wish someone in authority would please tell me what I saw that night," he wrote. "But I'm sure myself that someone, probably the government, sure knew what was going on at that time. If anyone can tell me the truth of what it was, without just guessing, I would sure like to know!"

Current Sighting Reports

In Hartsville, South Carolina, on Saturday night, May 8, 1999, one witness reports that at approximately 10:27 P.M. he and his sixteen-year-old niece watched an unidentified boomerang-shaped object glide over his father-in-law's home while they were stargazing outside. The teenage girl saw the object first and suddenly exclaimed "Wow!" When the witness looked up after checking her direction of sight, he saw a "darker than night" boomerang-shaped shadow glide silently overhead.

Even though his field of view was brief, the outline was very distinct. The object had rounded edges, with seven yellow-gold lights lining the front edge: one at the point, three down each leg. The lights did not reflect from the object as if they had been recessed in the object instead of protruding from it.

The witness lost sight after the object passed over the roof of the house. The other witness, the teenage girl, saw a formation of V-shaped objects at approximately 40 degrees above the horizon. They were a dull gray, reflecting the city lights in the distance from below. The patterns had the shape of concave arcs on the front and convex arcs on the back.

In nearby Georgia, a UFO researcher describes an encounter between flying triangles and jet interceptors. Were the planes part of a test of a secret military weapon system, or was this an intruder aircraft whose presence aroused the air defense command? The researcher reports that on March 10, 1999, at around 9:30 P.M. local time, a middle-aged horticulturist was driving southwest in Troup County along I-85 when a brilliant white ball passed in front of him. Flying extremely low and level and heading northwest, the nonblinking, seemingly solid white ball was the apparent size of Venus as seen from Earth. The white ball did not seem to be burning or falling as would a meteor. Rather, it appeared to be navigating, flying at nearly twice the speed of a small jet aircraft that was following it.

The witness estimated that the UFO and the small jet were flying at an altitude of less than 1,000 feet and took five to six seconds to cross the horizon in front of him. The jet had a triangle configuration of green and red lights, with at least one light blinking (as is required by the FAA). On arriving at the location where the white ball and small jet crossed I-85, the horticulturist heard the familiar *whop-whop-whop* of a low-flying helicopter pass directly overhead. The helicopter, based on its noise, seemed to be chasing the plane and ball.

A few nights later in the same area, on March 15, at dusk, a witness saw a brilliant white light appear overhead for nearly seven to eight minutes. Walking toward the woods about seventy-five yards away along with other members of his family, the witness heard what sounded like a humming sound that became louder until it sounded like a small roaring jet engine. Flying slowly, a black triangle with what appeared to be a five- to seven-foot wingspan flew about twenty feet above the witness. At 7:50 P.M., while looking again to the northeast, he saw a red light shoot straight up from the wood line. A family member who accompanied him into the woods saw a thin yellow beam about fifteen feet long instantly materialize and then disappear only thirty feet above them. Then, thirty seconds later, what the witnesses describe as a "blue invisible" triangle, the same size as the black triangle they had seen earlier but this time "riding" on a solid blue haze, streaked by at the same low height going to the northeast. It was flying at a blinding speed but without a sound. The witnesses could see the outline of the triangle clearly against the sky, but it seemed that the body of the triangle was transparent because they could see the night sky shining through it.

These triangle appearances were part of a series of observations of strange objects that took place over the county over a three- to four-day period. To this day, the witnesses still don't know what they saw.

European Sightings

Flying triangles caused a stir when they appeared over the skies of Belgium during the late 1980s. Unlike the United States sightings, which were (except for the Phoenix Lights) largely ignored by a UFO-weary media, the triangles sightings along the French-Belgian border drew photographers. Later sightings appeared in dramatic nighttime television in a recording made by one of the witnesses. The intensity of public interest increased to the point where even the prestigious Agence France Presse sought out the help of French ufologists to help explain the phenomenon that was now being witnessed in scores of small cities and towns near the French-Belgian border.

In one particular incident a researcher reported that a large triangular object with softened or rounded edges showed condensation trails as it flew at an altitude below 1,000 feet and circled very, very slowly overhead. Some witnesses reported that the object behaved almost as if it was looking for something as it flew over one small town, then disappeared and reappeared over a neighboring village. The object, which had steadily shining red and white lights, seemed to have actually landed in a village and left imprint traces on the grass before it took off.

Attempts to get radar tracking information from French air controllers were unsuccessful, according to the ufologists who contacted the Air Traffic Control Center. The center claimed that it could only track those objects that had their transponders turned on. French ufologists dismissed this explanation as ludicrous; transponders only transmit the flight's identity on the radar tracking system. Objects without transponders or with transponders turned off simply appear as unidentified blips. Over NATO countries, unidentified blips that behave unlike traditional aircraft and hover over a host country's airspace are often assumed to be hostile and generate an intercept from that country's military forces. The fact that these objects didn't seem to pose a threat or generate any response might mean, according to researchers, that they're familiar-looking UFOs which the military simply allows to intrude or that they're military flights themselves, a new aircraft being tested over NATO countries.

Characteristics of the Flying Triangles

The overwhelming majority of eyewitnesses to these phenomena report the same characteristics. The aircraft is huge, some people calling it the size of a football field and others saying it's larger than a 747 or an air force Galaxy cargo plane. When the aircraft flies below

1,000 feet, it seems to blot out the sky, especially at night. The black shape is defined by lights along its leading and trailing edges and in the moonlight casts a long, dark, moon shadow under the night sky.

Because of the flying wing outline that witnesses see, the aircraft reminds them of photos of stealth fighters they've seen in magazines. Some witnesses describe the aircraft in terms of boomerangs instead of triangles, reminiscent of the flying wing shapes that were developed as early as the 1930s and which were flown by both the Axis and the Allies during and after World War II. And if local airports had been telling the truth when they report, in response to the visual sightings, that there were no strange signatures on flight control radars, it could be that the aircraft were just like the stealth fighters and bombers in that they were either invisible to radar or able to evade radar tracking. However, if they were truly extraterrestrial spacecraft, it could well be that they, too, are designed to be invisible to both civilian and military radars.

Some observers are adamant that the aircraft they witnessed were triangular-shaped. Others have said they look more like flying wings or flying boomerangs. Still others, especially if we include the 1947 observation made by Kenneth Arnold, describe the shape they see floating through the air not as a triangle but as a flat, wide crescent. All of the shapes—the flying wing, the flying boomerang, the crescent, and the triangle—have at some point been incorporated or combined into different generations of military test aircraft.

If witnesses had seen the triangular aircraft cruising at normal aircraft speeds and at altitudes where people

Copy Rights W.P. Seidenburg

Courtesy William Seidenburg.

An artist's conception of the Roswell spaceship that crashed in 1947. It is more of a crescent or triangle than a flying saucer and it forms the basis, according to the artist, of the "lifting body" design of the SR-71 surveillance aircraft and the flying wing designs of the F-111 and B-2 bomber.

are accustomed to seeing planes fly, it is unlikely that the sightings would have caused any stir. The aircraft would have behaved like strange-looking planes and probably would have been so characterized. However, the ability of these aircraft to float at low altitudes, to hover, to make hairpin turns, and to fly silently at low speeds makes them seem more than unusual to anyone familiar with the flight characteristics of conventional aircraft. For those people who lived near air bases or who were in the military and had the chance to see various types of military aircraft, even the experimental stealths, these slow-moving triangles were bizarre-looking because they didn't perform like airplanes. Accordingly, witnesses began to describe these craft as UFOs because no traditional aircraft were capable of what these could do.

Superlifters and Delta Blimps: The Real Flying Triangles?

If one were to describe a craft that was the size of a football field or two, moved without a sound, seemed to float through the air and blot out the night sky behind it, and could climb vertically and change direction on a dime, that person might be describing a highly maneuverable blimp if it weren't for the triangular shape. But if it was discovered that an aircraft manufacturer was building and testing a delta- or crescent-shaped superlifter craft that had the buoyancy characteristics of a blimp combined with tilt rotors that generated the pulsating sound of a helicopter when they were angled at a steep pitch for maximum vertical lift, and also gave the craft the ability to hover, it might describe at least some of the craft that people have been seeing for the past ten years.

Moreover, if it were also revealed that such a craft

had actually been tested clandestinely for the past decade, flown in formations, operated over populated areas primarily at night, escorted by other stealth aircraft, and had the capacity to move over a million pounds of cargo, it would make sense that such a craft wasn't an extraterrestrial UFO at all, but a very advanced cargo plane.

In fact, Mickey Blackwell, an executive at Lockheed Martin, has revealed that the company has been building a blimp/plane it calls the Aerocraft since the early 1990s at its Skunkworks division. Skunkworks was the home of some of the air force's most advanced surveillance aircraft and its Stealth fighter and B-2 bomber, and has been producing top secret projects since the early 1960s.

Built in response to the military's need for a super cargo carrier that could move significant numbers of troops and equipment from home bases in the United States to frontlines anywhere in the world in forty-eight to seventy-two hours, the superblimp would have commercial viability as well. This flying wing, like any other dual-purpose aircraft, is also designed to operate as a business. In this case it could become the ultimate cargo hauler for commercial freight carriers such as UPS and the U.S. Postal Service, who would actually be the primary market for the Aerocraft.

The superblimp didn't just come into being overnight. It and other triangular-shaped military experimental aircraft have been in development for years, as early as the late 1940s when the first designs were brought back to the United States from a defeated Germany. And while the military development of triangular aircraft may explain some, or even the majority, of the sightings over the Hudson Valley, Phoenix, Southern California, and Europe, the question is why keep it a secret? What might lie behind the flying wing design that's made it such an ongoing secret for the past fifty years? To figure this out, we have to go back to the history of flying wing aircraft and their appearances over test ranges and populated areas.

Sightings of Other Triangular Aircraft

Since the late 1980s in areas around air force test ranges in the southwestern United States, observers have spotted various triangle or boomerang-shaped flying wings on what looked like simple test flights. In some cases, observers watched these wing-shaped craft taking off and landing from unidentified air bases where classified military projects were in development in Nevada and California or gliding over test ranges in western states. In some cases, these aircraft were followed by Stealth F-117 fighters, whose engines were reported to be louder than those of the craft they trailed. They had larger wingspans than the fighters, but without the telltale bat wing trailing edge. This, according to witnesses, eliminated the B-2 Stealth bomber as a candidate, although these flying wings might have been B-2 prototypes.

People who have had access to air force bases in the west have reported seeing large, black, triangular-shaped planes in hangars as early as the 1960s. With recessed engine inlets and rounded wing surfaces, these planes might have been test versions of the flat triangular shape that would come to dominate advanced prototype warplanes of the 1980s and 1990s, including some models such as the navy's A-12 and the F-22, whose development programs have recently been canceled or shrunk by the government.

Another type of triangular aircraft finding its way into UFO reports is what some witnesses have called the "pulsers," black or dark gray triangles whose engines operate with a pulsing or throbbing sound and which emit a vapor contrail in bursts, looking like sausage links, that seem to correlate with the pulsing. Different from the silent floaters, these craft—which according to some aviation technology experts may be capable of hypersonic speed—started appearing in the early-morning skies over Edwards Air Force Base in California in the late 1980s and over Nevada throughout 1990.

People who watched these objects flying over the Pacific Ocean test range north of Santa Barbara were impressed by the aircraft's speed, seemingly beyond the speed of current warplanes in the U.S. military arsenal. Airline pilots who fly the coastal routes have often seen these fast-moving planes at especially high altitudes out of the corridor of commercial air traffic. After they fly their test patterns, they skirt the air force and naval air bases in California where they would likely be observed and return to bases in Nevada, probably in the area of Groom Lake. Witnesses said they identified these planes more by their distinctive engine sound than by sight, especially during darkness when they were not easily observed.

There are lots of rumors circulating about this pulsing engine aircraft. Some people identify it as the Aurora, the mysterious hypersonic craft slated to replace U-2 and SR-71 reconnaissance planes. Others claim it to be the first operational version of what the air force

Courtesy William Seidenburg.

A front view of the SR-71 showing the similarities between the triangular lifting body shape of the fuselage and the artist's conception of the Roswell craft.

hopes will be its space plane, which takes off and lands like a conventional aircraft but which is able to achieve a low orbit. Rumored to be capable of speeds as high as 4,500 miles per hour, or Mach 6, the aircraft's Pulse Detonation Wave Engine is known for its distinctive contrail. One of the rumors surrounding the Aurora is that parts of the design concept for the plane, perhaps even the engine, were reverse-engineered from downed extraterrestrial UFOs. However, these are only rumors.

History of Triangular and Wing-Shaped Aircraft

Most people believe that the history of aircraft design is an open book. We can trace the development of aeronautical technology from the Wright brothers' first plane through the biplane, warplanes of World War II, the great commercial jetliners that came into service in the late

1950s and early '60s to the stealth aircraft of today. Yet almost on a parallel course until the stealth fighter and bomber became operational was the development of the flying wing or flying triangle aircraft, which took place largely in secret. These exotic flying wing, boomerang, and triangular-shaped aircraft have been around since 1919 when Alfred Lawson, an aircraft designer and pioneer, first patented the idea. But their development has remained in the shadows, causing some UFO researchers to speculate on a possible ET connection. Were flying wings modeled on extraterrestrial spacecraft that have been around since the turn of the century?

According to documents at the U.S. Patent Office the flying wing was an idea developed right here on Earth. Alfred Lawson, father of the flying wing, foresaw his design as the progenitor of generations of warplanes. He predicted that airplanes would fly nonstop across the Atlantic by 1930—a feat that Lindbergh accomplished in 1927—and that by the time airlines were a commercial enterprise air corridors and flight roadways through the sky would have to be established by some governing body to help control the traffic patterns.

His flying wing design, Lawson predicted, would be able to fly to the very edges of the atmosphere and could be sustained in flight for long periods of time. Most of his predictions have already come true, most remarkably the Lockheed flying triangle "superblimp," which is designed to spend long periods in the air as a transport, perhaps even as a high-altitude surveillance aircraft and enemy satellite killer during wartime.

Lawson's friend, Vincent Burnelli, carried on his work and developed a prototype flying wing called the RB-2,

which he tried to sell to the government as a bomber
just before America entered World War II. For a variety
of political reasons, President Roosevelt ordered that the
contract be pulled back, and it wasn't until the late 1940s
that the Lawson/Burnelli concepts turned up in U.S. Air
Force bomber designs and then again twenty years later
in designs for the Stealth prototypes.

The German Flying Wing

Innovative aircraft designers were also at work in Germany, where flying wings were prototyped as early as
the 1920s by Alfred Lippisch. In Tim Matthews's book,
UFO Revelation, a developmental history of secret technologies, he describes the German evolution of flying
wings and boomerangs from the Lippisch glider designs
of the 1920s to the early jet engines being designed for
the Luftwaffe in the 1930s as Germany rearmed in preparation for war, and through the war years themselves.
The Germans actually possessed triangular-shaped jet
aircraft before the end of the war and even rocket-
propelled delta winged aircraft that were never deployed.
The Lippisch-designed rocket plane was obtained by the
United States by the end of the war and became one of
the secret development programs during the 1940s and
1950s as we raced against the Soviets to deploy the next
generation of exotic aircraft.

The Horten brothers also developed flying wing technology in Nazi Germany during World War II and, in
1945, saw the test flight of their turbo-jet powered flying wing. The Luftwaffe was already deploying jet fight-

ers against American bombers by the last months of the war, driving the Allies to get their hands on the technology before the Soviets did. Finally, the Americans overran the Horten facility in April 1945 and took possession of an aircraft that was to drive U.S. and British designers for the ensuing fifty years.

Flying Wings after World War II

The next flying wing design to become operational was the U.S. Air Force YB-49, more a boomerang shape than a triangle, that was flying at just about the time that pilot Kenneth Arnold reported his mysterious sighting over the Cascade Mountains in Washington in 1947. Although he is reputed to have coined the word "flying saucer," authors Tim Matthews, in *UFO Revelation*, and Peter Sturrock, in *The UFO Enigma*, explain that he did nothing of the kind. He merely reported seeing a crescent-shaped craft flying through the air as if someone had thrown a saucer.

Moreover, Arnold never believed he was looking at an extraterrestrial craft. On the contrary, he said he thought they were United States military test aircraft in the shape of flying crescents. Yet his report triggered five decades of flying saucer sightings and may have been behind Colonel Blanchard's instructions to his Public Information Officer at the 509th Army Airfield in Roswell, New Mexico, when he ordered Lieutenant Walter Haut to tell the press, after the crash of a strange craft in the desert, that the army had recovered a "flying saucer." (It was the press release that sparked the nationwide fascination with flying saucers for the next two decades, and to this very day Walter Haut will tell anyone who visits him at the International UFO Museum in Roswell, New Mexico, that the words "flying saucer" came directly out of Colonel Blanchard's own mouth.)

We believe we know from eyewitnesses to the Roswell crash retrieval that the craft wasn't really a circular saucer at all but a crescent that bears an uncanny resemblance to the Horten aircraft and the flying wing prototypes that made their appearances in the 1970s. This resemblance has led to two different paths of speculation. First, was it only a test aircraft that crashed outside of Roswell, a test aircraft so secret and important that the army would rather have the Soviets believe we'd been visited by a flying saucer than been caught out in the open with an aircraft both sides were trying to develop? By first releasing and then denying a crash of a flying saucer, especially by describing it as a weather balloon, was American Army Intelligence trying to outfox the Soviets, who, the army knew, had thoroughly penetrated the civilian intelligence services?

On the other hand, do the reports of alien bodies, aircraft components and pieces of fabric with strange properties, and the extraordinarily long development curve for flying wing technology over the next forty years lend some credence to the appearance of an extraterrestrial craft whose components might have stimulated research into flying wing and exotic technologies over the ensuing decades? Might not the Germans, according to reports that persisted right through the postwar years, have stumbled upon extraterrestrial technologies and used them to enhance their own experiments with flying wing shapes? And could this have accounted for the absolute secrecy the Americans imposed on their own flying wing aircraft through the postwar years right through the 1980s?

Whether extraterrestrial or homegrown, the flying wing aircraft was in development for the military as early as 1947, with the Northrop YB-49 bomber flying over the southwest by 1948. The YB-49 program was canceled by the Pentagon in 1952, however, and all models were ordered destroyed. Some have suggested the reason was that the YB-49s contained alien technology from the Roswell crash. Other people have suggested a far more mundane explanation having to do with the air force's delivery of the flying wing design information to other aircraft manufacturers for the purpose of combining the design with stealth technology to create the next generation of military aircraft.

If experimentation and prototyping began in the 1960s and was stimulated by sophisticated computer modeling capabilities in the 1970s, it's not far-fetched that at least some of the flying triangle sightings of the 1960s through the 1970s can be accounted for. By 1980 the air force already had flying "proof of concept" aircraft to show that the flying wing design was viable. However, because these were top secret projects, sightings of these aircraft received no official response from the air force other than denials, while the CIA, according to its own history of its involvement with UFOs, actively used the American public's fascination with flying saucers to encourage the belief that secret air force planes were UFOs.

In this way they actively engaged in a cover-up, albeit of classified aircraft rather than UFOs.

But even this doesn't explain the complete range of flying triangle sightings witnesses have reported. Were it not for the overwhelming size of the objects, the ability of the objects to accelerate almost instantly to hypersonic speeds, and the strange glowing orbs that navigate independently around the edges of the triangles, docking and undocking at will, maybe all of the flying triangle sightings can be explained away as highly classified aircraft. But the number of witnesses who've claimed sightings of triangular-shaped objects that seem beyond the technological development curve of even our most advanced aircraft is too great to be ignored. Maybe, for the greater part of the twentieth century, flying triangle UFOs have played a far greater role in the development of aeronautical technology than our governments are willing or able to disclose.

CHAPTER 3

The "Russian Roswell" and Other Cases from Inside Russia

"How much easier his task and mine would be in these meetings that we held if suddenly there was a threat to this world from another species outside in the universe."

President Ronald Reagan, speaking of Chairman Mikhail Gorbachev of the Soviet Union at the Geneva Summit, 1985

THE UFO FILES OF THE FORMER SOVIET UNION, KEPT top secret until Glasnost by the Russian military and the KGB, are now being released by Russian UFO researchers over the Internet and to organizations like the Mutual UFO Network (MUFON). They are fascinating to Western ufologists because they provide a whole other perspective on UFOs. In the United States, UFO incidents—when they are not kept top secret by the military—are officially derided as either curiosities, mass hallucinations, or hoaxes. In some of the Russian UFO files, however, the encounters are treated as deadly serious threats, especially when it comes to military encounters with flying objects.

What secrets do the Russian flying saucer files contain? Are they mirror images of UFO encounters reported in the West, or do they reflect a different type of UFO experience? For military analysts the KGB files may contain treasure troves of information about how the Russian military reacts to intrusions of its airspace and what tactics Russian aircraft and naval vessels follow to intercept a perceived threat. Among the cases is the story of the "Russian Roswell," the 1991 pursuit of a cylindrical UFO by Russian fighters and the object's crash landing at the edge of the Tien Shan mountain range in central Asia. The pursuit, the crash, and the near decade's worth of attempts to reach the site and retrieve the debris are one of the most exciting stories to come out of the annals of Russian UFO experiences.

The story of the mysterious object over the Caspian Sea was told by ufologists Nikolay Subbotin and Emil Bachurin of RUFORS, the Russian UFO Research Station, who reported the story in *UFO Magazine* in collaboration with American UFO researcher Bill Hamilton. Emil Bachurin was more than one of the story's reporters, however. He was a member of an expedition to the remote and desolate crash site. He claims to have seen the actual craft and photographed it, as well as sketched hand diagrams of the object. Nikolay Subbotin headed an expedition in 1998 to visit the crash site. But by the time they had reached the area, the UFO was gone, and it seemed to Subbotin as though the site had been scrubbed clean of any remains of the downed craft.

The Spacecraft

The incident began on August 28, 1991, at just before 4:45 P.M. A large object almost 600 meters long and 110 meters in diameter appeared over the Caspian Sea, showing up as an unidentified image on the radar screens of a tracking station on the Mangyshlak peninsula. Flying at a speed of 9,600 kilometers per hour (6,336 mph) at an altitude of 6,600 meters (21,653 feet), the object did not return a transponder signal on radar. Concerned now that what they saw on their screens was an intruder in sensitive airspace, the operators at the tracking station broadcast their standard friend-or-foe identification requests to the object streaking overhead. But it returned no answer. In the silence following their repeated radio transmissions, the radar operators classified it as an unknown and went to the next stage before calling in a hostile aircraft intrusion alert.

They first checked with the nearby cosmodrome at Kapustin Yar to see whether this was a launch vehicle from their facility. Maybe the spaceport had staged an unscheduled test that would explain the object now soaring over the area. But the officer at Kapustin Yar who picked up the phone told them that there were no tests of any kind under way. Then he added that his radar equipment was showing the object as well. Now the operators at Mangyshlak had a confirming sighting from a nearby facility. There was no doubt there was something there.

Mangyshlak didn't waste any time. They went to military alert. They made an immediate report of the contact and confirmation to the area air defense command, which diverted two MIG 29 fighters from a regular patrol route to intercept the object and scrambled an additional pair of MIGs from aerodrome K. If the object seemed to be a craft under direct pilot control, the fighters were ordered to force it to land at aerodrome K. If it refused to obey orders or resisted in any way, the MIGs were authorized to fire on it and shoot it down.

As military flight controllers computed the direction and speed of the object, they triangulated possible intercept vectors and agreed on an interception point along the coast of the Aral Sea. They then issued the *execute* command. Accordingly, shortly before 5:15 P.M., just over the western coastline of the Aral Sea, the Russian fighters picked the object up on radar.

As they closed to visual range, they saw what looked like a large, gray, cigar-shaped dirigible partially defined by the afternoon sunlight. The flight leader initiated a standard friend-or-foe protocol, radioing the strange craft for identification and ordering it to reduce speed and take up position inside the formation behind the leading MIG. Again the flying cylinder was silent, did not transmit any identifiers or transponder codes, and did not comply with the flight leader's orders. Nor did the object seem to be taking any evasive action, allowing the formation of interceptors to fly around it and observe its odd, tubular shape, matte gray coloring, and two circular portholes near the rounded tip in the front.

As they flew in a rough formation alongside the object, the MIGs waited for instructions from the ground and kept a close watch on the object's movements, just in case it tried to break away or take hostile action. At a quick emergency staff meeting at the area air defense

Courtesy RUFORS.

RUFORS 1998

"Russian Roswell." An artist's conception of the UFO that crashed in the Tien Shan mountains.

base, Russian air force officers held a conference about the object their fighters now had under close visual surveillance. Should they blow it out of the sky? No, they decided, at least not right away. Maybe if they fired warning shots across its path, they could force it down, see who was inside, and study the technology.

"Close in from either side," the group commander ordered his fighters in the air. "Fly parallel to the target and fire warning shots in its path." Maybe that would make it comply with the orders to land, the Russian commanders thought.

The MIGs responded, tightening the formation around the flying cylinder as they moved in from a distance of 800 to 500 meters (1,640 feet). As they got closer, the pilots noticed that the cylinder had what looked like a set of green symbols or characters around its tail, although they could not decipher the markings. The pilots armed their weapons and prepared to fire.

Suddenly, as they depressed their triggers, it seemed as if the MIGs' fire control systems experienced a complete electrical failure. Nothing worked. The buttons were useless. Then the pilots' cockpit control panels went dead, and radio communication was cut off. Finally, the planes' jet engines began to sputter and the cylindrical object surged ahead of them.

Without radar, radio, or even navigational controls, the planes were helpless in the air. Ground radars tracked the object assuming a zigzag course back over the Aral Sea and increasing its speed to an astonishing 68,000 kilometers per hour (42,000 mph) while climbing vertically and then dropping to an altitude of 4,500 meters (14,763 feet) back over civilian airspace.

Suddenly the radios in the MIGs began to crackle and power returned to the cockpit controls. The pilots were ordered to reestablish control of their jets as soon as they could, break off their pursuit of the object, and nurse their aircraft back to the aerodrome. Meanwhile flight controllers at Mangyshlak notified civilian and air force personnel along the object's apparent route that an unidentified craft was traveling through their areas that could pose a collision threat to other aircraft. However, just before 5:30 P.M., the object disappeared from all radars just as quickly as it had appeared. And that, everyone presumed at the time, was the end of the story.

RUFORS © 1998

Courtesy RUFORS.

Another view of the Tien Shan UFO.

The Crash

About a month after the sighting and encounter, near the end of September 1991, strange rumors began circulating among the residents of the villages surrounding Karakol that a large object had crashed deep in the mountains to the east. Inside a region called Shaitan Mazar, or the Devil's Grave, there were stories about a huge, seemingly fabricated object that had fallen out of the sky and broke into pieces against a craggy hillside near the headwaters of the Sary Dzhaz river. Within the next ten days, an experienced search and rescue team—including mountain climbers and investigators led by Anton Bogatov, chairman of SAKKUFON, the UFO research group—had been organized into an expedition to locate and mark the crash site, take photographs, retrieve any artifacts that could be studied, and try to determine the nature of the object that had crashed. Could it have been a UFO, or was it a meteor or piece of asteroid that had survived reentry?

Shaitan Mazar, in the Tien Shan mountains along the border of Kyrgyzstan and Kazakhstan, is of great significance to the history of Asia because it lies astride the medieval spice and silk trading routes between China and Islamic territories in Asia. During the history of the Soviet Union in the twentieth century, the entire region was kept closed to foreign visitors by the Soviet government, and the Kyrgyz, its mysterious people who are descended from Mongols, remained shrouded in mystery amid the shadows of the fog-shrouded and snow-capped Tien Shan mountains. It was into this remote area that the expedition traveled to locate the crash site.

The group trekked through the snows of the Tien Shan mountains for over two weeks, following rumors and the directions of the locals, but couldn't find the crash site. They finally determined that the site lay at the other end of a narrow mountain pass that would take them through the Sary Dzhaz river valley to the isolated head of the river. The steep valley walls were piled high with snowdrifts that teetered precariously over the edge of the cliffs and threatened to obliterate any expedition in a sudden avalanche. Less than a month after they started out, the group, some of whom were either injured or suffering from exposure or frostbite, made their way back to a camp in Bishek where they stayed for a while before heading home.

The June 1992 Expedition

News of the object's crash in the region continued to spread over the winter and into the new year, especially among official circles. Local residents said that it was something unearthly that gave burns to whomever approached the area and even, some said, made watches stop dead. But these were only rumors passed by mouth among residents of the local villages.

At the same time, SAKKUFON had received information that the Russian Air Force had located the remote location of the crash site in November of 1991 and had made at least one attempt to retrieve the object using a helicopter to try to hoist it out. But amid the snow and confined area at the site the attempt failed and the helicopter crashed to the valley floor. There were no survivors, and the air force was planning no future attempts as the Russian winter closed in over Central Asia. This gave SAKKUFON time to plan a land-based expedition which, they hoped, would reach the crash site before the military moved in. It was a race.

SAKKUFON began its expedition by recruiting a crew of volunteers, all experts in their respective scientific fields who had been prepared by team leaders and trainers psychologically as well as physically for the trek. They passed compatibility and stress tests as well as physical endurance exercises and survival techniques. Rather than approach the crash site in one column, Major German G. Svechkov (retired), the expedition's leader, broke the retrieval crew into three separate teams, now with mountain climbing training to help them. This time, the teams were better prepared than the first expedition and better equipped as well.

In June of 1992 they started from a camp about two kilometers (1¼ miles) from where they believed the crash site to be and scaled the northern slope of one of the mountains. They planned extensive reconnaissance of the area before setting up camp at the crash site, to make sure the radiation levels were safe and that the teams would be able to survive an encounter with an object that might still be emitting its own highly charged force field. No one really knew what to expect when they reached the object, but they wanted to make sure they weren't walking into certain death.

By the middle of June the groups had moved out from their base camp and discovered the object. It had come to rest on a long flat plateau and lay in two pieces, as if it had broken right down the middle either when it attempted to land or had collided with the mountain above. Yet, as one of the expedition members has described it, there it was, obviously an object from another world, and still generating some form of energy field.

You could feel it all around you, expedition member Emil Bachurin reported. The team that approached was almost overcome with a sense of fear, psychological dread, and physical anxiety that put all of them on edge. The anxiety turned to a feeling of hopelessness and extreme fatigue as they crept nearer to what now seemed to them clearly to be a UFO. As they approached to a distance of 1,000 meters, they could feel the electricity in the air, static electricity that threw their instruments off and made their precision electronic devices useless. Dials on compasses veered away from true north and locked onto the object, and other meters simply went dead and registered zero.

But even from a distance of a thousand meters away the observers could figure out how the object must have crashed. It had hit an overhanging rocky ledge and then exploded from the inside, blowing apart its external plating. And now it was lying in two pieces with the metal showing the stress from an internal explosion.

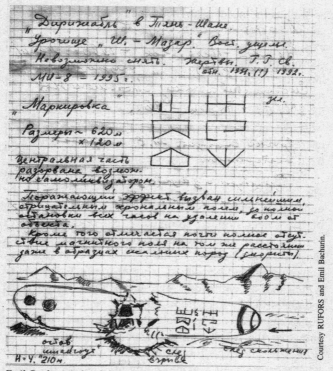

Emil Bachurin's hand-drawn notes and diagram of the crash site as he saw it on the first expedition into the Tien Shan mountains.

The force field of static electricity was so intense it made the hair on the expedition members' bodies stand straight up, even through layers of outdoor clothing in the chilly June temperatures that clung to the ground in the high mountain passes and river valleys. And the magnetic field around the object threw off all metallic dials, as well as the needles on the compasses. While observers could see that the object was lying along an east-west axis, the compass needles returned a false reading and showed the object lying on a true north-south axis. Similarly, the magnetometers showed that there was an intense magnetic field defined by the shape of the craft itself. At the same time, objects lying outside the space craft's field were devoid of any magnetic readings. It was as if the energy surrounding the craft had completely demagnetized the area by absorbing energy into its own field.

Whatever energy field was generated by the object also affected all of the clocks and chronometers on the expedition. Those clocks which were in a line of sight of the object stopped completely and reset themselves to zero. Even when they were removed from the area, they could not be reset to the correct time because they kept stopping. Other clocks were also affected, some of which lost an entire day. The anomaly so intrigued the members of the expedition that they kept repeating experiments with backup clocks and chronometers to make sure that the results were consistent from day to day. Some of the expedition's members began to wonder whether time itself was not being affected by the object and that what they thought was a slowing down of clocks was really a temporal distortion field in which time itself was slowing down. Similar temporal anomalies had been reported at other UFO sites where objects had either crashed or landed.

Among the other instruments that failed to operate at the crash site were quartz generators and portable power supplies. When the scientists attempted to run wiring to power the equipment that would measure electronic fields and frequencies around the object, the generators burned up the instant they were switched on. All further attempts to run a portable power generator for the field equipment were similarly unsuccessful and only indicated that what looked like an inert object split into two pieces on the hard plateau was actually a powerful source of energy propagating a strange type of field that caused other energy supplies to burn up.

Without the ability to carry out electronic measurements and lacking sufficient cable to run power lines from well outside the grip of the object's energy field, the expedition members were left to develop their theories based on visual observation and the hand measurements they were able to take at the scene. They speculated that the cylinder had been moving at a very high rate of speed, possibly fleeing from the MIGs, when the underside of its fuselage hit and bounced off the rocky ledge they could see above them, which was about 1,500 meters, or almost 5,000 feet, away from the spot where the craft finally came to rest. The object skidded along the hard ground and ruptured, causing an internal explosion at some point during the skid. They couldn't determine whether the object came to a stop before exploding or exploded as soon as it touched the ground.

From what they could tell, the explosion took place right in the midsection of the craft, bending the metal out and creating a funnel shape where the hull blew open. The nose of the cylinder was dented, and the cracks in the nose looked as though they were caused by the object's impact with the ground. There were other cracks and damage as well, particularly on the left side of the cylinder, which appeared to have bounced and

An exploded view of Emil Bachurin's description of the interior of the crashed Tien Shan UFO.

then dragged along the ground. Or the damage could have been caused by the explosion.

Perhaps the most mysterious aspect of the craft, Nikolay Subbotin wrote in his report, were the bizarre green symbols around the tail of the craft's fuselage. The scientists at the crash site couldn't translate the symbols. They certainly didn't appear to be either Cyrillic or Arabic, nor were they hieroglyphics, which the scientists believed they could have recognized, if not translated. They were markings of some sort, possibly identifiers just like the symbols on our own aircraft, arranged and organized around the tail of the craft just before a series of rings around the stern.

Although they couldn't approach the aircraft any closer than 800 meters (2,624 feet), where an energy barrier shut down their instruments and made the men feel weak and demoralized, the scientists reported that they believed the rings to be part of some propulsion engine. And from what they could make out through the damaged hull, there seemed to have been internal beams and horizontal flooring, indicating that the craft might have different levels, like the decks on a submarine, and could have even contained a crew. There were no signs of life, however, nor could the observers make out any bodies. From what they could see at the site, the expedition members couldn't determine whether there had been any crew at all or whether the entire craft was a remotely piloted device, similar to the unmanned surveillance drones that the United States deployed during the air war over Kosovo. But before they left the crash site, the scientists were able to copy the symbols from the tail of the craft and get a closer look inside to see its interior decks.

The members of the expedition took lots of photos, but, according to Emil Bachurin, the radiation at the scene apparently overexposed the film at the same time it caused radiation burns on some of the personnel, including Bachurin, who wrote the report that later appeared in *UFO Magazine* along with his drawings of the object. The intense magnetic and electrical fields also wiped out the magnetic videotape cartridges they'd brought with them, and caused the shutters and electrical motors on the video cameras to malfunction as well. The cameras and film behaved just like the rest of their instruments and failed, as if a damping field around the object shut down every device that was brought too close to it.

In the distance, the expedition could also see the wreckage of the Russian MI-8 helicopter that had tried to retrieve the object, but they couldn't find any bodies of crew members and didn't know if another rescue team had removed the bodies. Had the helicopter crashed because its instruments failed when it tried to enter the field? If so, the military would have a hard time removing this object.

The August 1998 Expedition

Although the expedition that reached the crash site in June 1992 claims to have actually seen the craft, and Bachurin was able to make sketches of it, the green symbols along its tail, and details of the bracing frames inside the exploded hull, scientific measurements were lacking due to instrument failure. Expedition leaders realized afterward that they needed to measure and diagram the magnetic field around the object to see what shape it took. Would it follow the same general outline of the craft, or would it look like a three-dimensional cone in which the antimagnetic readings would get stronger toward the center? Would the field operate like a magnetic black hole, demagnetizing everything around it with an increasing force toward a physical center? They also wanted to define the borders of the gravitational field around the object and map the temporal distortion field as well. Bachurin and Subbotin theorized that the expedition might have stumbled over a phenomenon described by physicists in which time is actually distorted as waves or particles approach the perimeter, or event horizon, of a black hole. If this was the effect around the object it would be a major scientific discovery.

The reports of the 1992 expedition to the crash site as well as stories of the attempted recovery of the object by the Russian military were generating a considerable response among Russian UFO researchers. There were a number of stories about the crash of an experimental dirigible in the Tien Shan region as well as reports of an air force top secret remotely piloted surveillance vehicle that had crashed. Recovery of the vehicle from the inhospitable mountain river valley had become a priority because it was considered a dangerous source of radiation. One rumor suggested that an experimental dirigible had been equipped with a nuclear engine which exploded when the craft bounced off the ledge and hit the ground. Other rumors described the object as a nuclear-powered component for a new space station that had broken loose from a launch vehicle and cruised back to earth where it exploded and charged the area with radiation.

Fund-raising for a third trek to the crash site began within months after the 1992 expedition, but it took six years to assemble the personnel and money for a new visit. This time, researcher and author Nikolay Subbotin helped organize the expedition because, he wrote, he wanted to see firsthand what the site looked like and to verify the details of the UFO version of the story. He wrote that the flow of either misinformation or disinformation about the crash was so intense that another attempt to photograph the object, take the kinds of instrument readings Bachurin had suggested five years earlier, and collect soil samples was worth the expense and effort. If this was a UFO, it would be a find of extraordinary importance that would surpass Roswell and Bentwaters as a source of information about UFO crashes or landings.

But the Subbotin RUFORS expedition was plagued with problems from the start. They tried to enlist the aid of Major German G. Svechkov, leader of the 1992 expedition, but he didn't want to go: his son indicated that there were aspects about what was discovered on the 1992 expedition that made Major Svechkov nervous even six years later. With only a few thousand dollars from one of the backers of the first expedition, Subbotin and his RUFORS group set out on August 20, 1998, and after difficulties with local Kazakhstan officials, including the militia and the KGB, they decided to go to the site without any official permission. Traveling on land vehicles and on foot, the Subbotin expedition finally made camp near Shaitan Mazar, only a few kilometers away from the crash site. They rented a helicopter and found the site within twenty minutes, but the UFO was gone.

As the helicopter circled the crash site, Subbotin could make out what seemed like a landing strip on the flat ground. The large rocks that the first group had described seemed to have been crushed by earth-moving equipment that also smoothed out any traces of a UFO's having skidded across the terrain. What it looked like, Subbotin wrote, was that the site had been fully excavated and cleaned after all the debris, including the UFO, was removed. It reminded Subbotin of a landscaping and regrading operation because the dirt appeared fresh and unlike the earth on the overhanging hills. In fact, looking at what could only be a helipad, Subbotin thought he could have been looking at a military landing strip instead of a crash site.

Electrical instruments in the helicopter indicated none of the anomalies registered by the first expedition six years before. Perhaps it was only the object itself that had propagated the strange fields, and once the object was removed the electronic and magnetic traces disap-

peared along with it. In systematic flyovers Subbotin
could not get the magnetic instruments in the helicopter
to register in the ways Bachurin had described. And without film from the earlier expedition, no proof remained
that the object they were seeking had really been there
in the first place, except for the descriptions that
Bachurin had first given.

After his return to Moscow, Subbotin tried to rein-
terview members of the first expedition who had accompanied Emil Bachurin to Shaitan Mazar. German
Svechkov's son confirmed that his father had taken part
in the first trek, just as Anton Bogatov had confirmed
that he was one of the leaders of the 1992 expedition.
By comparing the stories of the two expedition members with the stories of Emil Bachurin, Subbotin convinced himself that the 1992 expedition was a real event
and that its members had evidently found something that
had been removed from the site. But what that object
was, he didn't know for sure. All he had were Emil
Bachurin's sketches, photographs of some of the burns
on Bachurin's body, and the story of how the scientific
instruments reacted to some kind of magnetic and gravitational field.

Why was the mysterious object removed and the site
scrubbed so thoroughly as to remove any traces of evidence that something had crashed there? Subbotin could
only surmise that if it had not been the crash of a UFO,
then it had to be something else that the military wanted.
Since Shaitan Mazar is close to the Russian border with
China, perhaps the air force was after one of its own
surveillance devices that it routinely used to watch Chinese troop movements, or maybe this wasn't a Russian

device at all, but an American unmanned surveillance probe that the Russians had actually managed to divert and force to crash into the mountain. If so, it would have been a treasure trove indeed, one that the military would have wanted to keep secret. However, in a country where UFO stories abound and where some have described battles between flying saucers and other unidentified craft, the crash of a strange cylinder at Shaitan Mazar ranks as one of Russia's greatest unsolved UFO mysteries.

The Battle of the Flying Saucers

Nikolay Subbotin cites a second major UFO incident. This one took place on September 16, 1989, in the skies over Zaostrovka, near the permafrost region of Russia. Six gray flying saucers, circular disks that seemed to fly in a rotational pattern, closed formation with each other and attacked a seventh, gold-hued, craft that was trying to escape. This battle, "right out of *Star Wars,*" as Subbotin described it, was witnessed by hundreds of people who stood there, transfixed, at the sight of spacecraft battling one another above a Russian port city. Witnesses marveled as the formation of six disks chased a seventh out of a cloud bank. As it tried to escape, the six flying saucers made hairpin turns, climbed steeply, and dropped to below 5,000 feet in the evening sky, shooting beams of light at the golden flying saucer, which also fired light beams as it took evasive maneuvers.

In his RUFORS Internet newsletter, Subbotin writes that a description of the air battle appeared in the local *Semipalatinsk* newspaper. It was written by a former

Russian helicopter commander in the Afghan war who said that the energy generated from the flying disks was so intense it shut down the power grid in Zaostrovka and plunged the city into darkness just as evening fell. "Workers watched with horror in their hearts," the witness said, as the combat raged over their heads. With their city completely blacked out, all the observers could do was watch the fight play out, just as if they were spectators at a football game, and comment on the unreal show going on above them. The helicopter commander, a man by the name of Sichenko, recorded the conversations of onlookers and wrote his article based, in part, on what the witnesses recorded at the scene.

Finally, the six saucers, forming a mushroomlike formation, with two of the craft guarding their undersides and four of the craft deployed in a wide circle, pursued the seventh and fired at it with some kind of energy beam. In the end, the gold-colored saucer couldn't escape the attack, was hit repeatedly with the weapon beam, and began to lose altitude. At first the saucer's fall seemed controlled, as if it were looking for a place to set down and escape the craft in pursuit. But it couldn't sustain its controlled descent and finally disappeared behind a house. The formation of six flying saucers seemed to establish a search pattern to look for the crash site approximately ten kilometers outside the port city. They then disappeared.

Subbotin writes that the saucer crashed in a bog on a military test range, a secured area that had long since been closed to civilians. Subbotin's group managed to visit the area in the autumn of 1990, but, as would happen in the Tien Shan crash, the area had been completely cleared and all evidence of any downed aircraft, identified or not, had been removed. Subbotin had been told that a military team had worked the isolated and partially flooded area prior to RUFORS's arrival and had experienced casualties. At least one of the men had received severe burns, a fact reportedly verified by Emil Bachurin, who had seen his medical chart.

Other workers on the removal team breached secrecy regarding the discovery and removal of the aircraft, possibly because they, too, had received radiation burns, and were punished by the chief of retrieval operations at the military base. Later, an unauthorized airplane piloted by a civilian tried to fly over the crash area to see whether any visual evidence of a downed flying saucer remained, but his instruments gave out as he approached the crash site and he had to veer off. He, too, was severely punished for flying over a restricted area.

Ultimately the entire test range was closed down, Subbotin reported, and its perimeter is tightly guarded. No one is allowed onto the base. Has it become a sealed grave site for a flying saucer that no human being can approach without experiencing radiation burns severe enough to cause almost certain death? The mystery of the downed flying saucer that may still remain in the bog is all the more intriguing because it may contain secrets about why it was engaged in a battle with other spaceships. Is there an ongoing battle among alien species in near space? Is Earth just another battleground in a war for our planet's natural or biological resources? Who out there are the protectors and who are the aggressors? Maybe if there really is a flying saucer buried within the swamps near the military base at Zaostrovka, it contains the answer.

Chapter 4

The Gulf Breeze Mystery

"I can assure you that flying saucers, given that they exist, are not constructed by any power on Earth."

President Harry Truman, White House press
conference, April 4, 1950

IF WE LOOK AT THE KINDS OF UFO ENCOUNTER CASES that have become famous over the years, we can see how they tend to fall into various categories. Some are simply sightings and yield no physical evidence. Some sighting events yield photos, such as the ones that appeared in the French COMETA report. Some are actual encounters with a craft, as in the Roswell and Bentwaters cases. Still others are abductions, such as the Betty and Barney Hill case, in which people report being brought under the control of some other entity. Rarely, a case brings together all of these elements, resulting in stunning photos and corroborating testimony from witnesses, and becomes a celebrated "event case." One such case was the Gulf Breeze sightings, UFO encounters that centered on a small residential community outside the huge military and naval complex in Pensacola, Florida, beginning in late 1987.

The Gulf Breeze Sightings

At first glance, Gulf Breeze, a small community in the Florida panhandle, would seem to be an unlikely setting for one of the most controversial series of UFO sightings in the past fifteen years. Yet, because Gulf Breeze is just across a narrow bay from the nuclear submarine base at Pensacola, Florida, and the naval air station, which is a flight training center for U.S. Navy pilots, it is actually located in an area of important military facilities. Gulf Breeze is also near Eglin Air Force Base, one of the most important military installations on the East Coast, and a short flight away from the Gulf Coast shipyards, which have been locations of other reported alien abductions. When most people thought about Gulf Breeze, they conjured up images of a conservative, middle-class southern community where the last thing anyone would expect would be for one of the local building contractors, Ed Walters, to report seeing a flying saucer floating above the treetops near his house. But that's exactly what happened in early November 1987.

In his book, *The Gulf Breeze Sightings* (1990), Ed Walters describes the first sighting as an almost innocuous event that began while he was sitting at the desk in his office in the front of his house. It was early in the evening, shortly after his wife, Frances, had driven out to pick up something from the store. Looking out at the tree in front of his house, Walters thought he saw the lights of an aircraft that might have been a navy helicopter, but he heard no sound from an engine. Viewing the craft through tree limbs, he wrote, he realized that the glowing blue and gray lights were not from a helicopter. In fact, they weren't from any type of craft he'd ever seen before, and he'd seen quite a variety flying over the area from the naval air station. He stepped out onto the front porch to get a better look at whatever this was and realized it was actually circular, with other lights besides the blue glow.

Realizing that this might possibly be what his rational mind was telling him it could not be, Walters ran back into the house and grabbed a nearby Polaroid camera that he usually carried to his job sites. He stepped out onto his front porch again to get another look at the strange craft. By that time it had moved out from behind the tree and he thought he could possibly snap a photo to prove to himself that he wasn't really crazy.

As the object moved farther into the clearing, Walters's mind kept recoiling from the reality he was seeing. The craft wasn't really spinning or rotating, it was just floating as if it were inside its own bubble. It didn't seem to rustle the trees or cause any aerial disturbance that he could make out. And it was quiet. It moved through the air without the sound of rushing wind, the noise of an engine, or even the hum of something electrical. And that's what made it seem so eerie as it moved out from behind the tree completely and seemed to float toward him, almost as if someone inside realized he was taking photos with his Polaroid.

As the object glided toward Walters's house at an altitude of approximately two hundred feet, Ed noticed

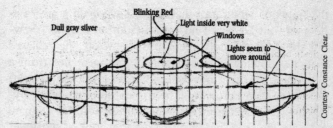

Gulf Breeze. An artist's eyewitness rendition of a flying saucer. The design is similar to the descriptions provided by Ed Walters in Gulf Breeze Sightings.

details about the craft that never turned up in the photos he took that night. He wrote that he could see what he thought were little windows, some of which were lit, evenly spaced around the main circular body of the craft. The object also seemed to have a large aperture beneath it as if it were the outlet of a huge engine. Walters reported that he wanted to get a picture of this as well and ran out into the street to get a better shot.

However, to his dismay, the craft almost immediately moved right over his head, swallowing the distance in a single heartbeat. No aircraft he'd ever seen moved like that. And as he looked directly up into the gaping bright white opening, he suddenly felt himself hit with the power of a force he'd never felt before. It wasn't painful, but when he tried to move his arms and hands, straining against a blue light that had suddenly enveloped him, he felt pain. His lungs, too, were constrained by whatever force this was, and he had to gulp for air in short, shallow breaths that hurt as if he were holding his breath underwater.

Now in a panic at what was happening to him and unable to move or to scream for help, he felt that his brain was encased in a frozen sculpture. He knew where he was, he never lost consciousness, but he simply couldn't move. As he struggled against the force pressing against him and fought to suck air into his lungs, he felt his feet being lifted off the ground. His whole body began to float, locked in the beam that was keeping him from moving. At this point, Walters wrote, the sensation was well beyond unpleasant, it was painful and terrifying. Something had gained complete control over his body and was moving him through the air against his will.

Walters felt, more than heard, voices inside his brain telling him not to resist, but he kept on fighting as a series of images of dogs played behind his eyes. Where were these images coming from? Were they being played back from his own brain to calm him down as whatever it was that was holding him captive was lifting him off the ground? As he tried to scream, to fight back against what could only be described as an abduction, he was suddenly dropped right to the pavement in the middle of the street. The blue light was gone.

Suddenly alone in the middle of the street amid the evening darkness, Walters looked around him and found the snapshots of the object his Polaroid had spit out before the craft captured him in its blue beam. He called out for help, but there was no answer. The silence was eerie. It was as if everyone in his neighborhood had gone to sleep when the object arrived overhead and stayed asleep despite all the commotion. Hearing no response from any of the neighbors, he crawled on the ground, retching from the physical and traumatic stress of the incident, trying not to throw up as he gathered the photos.

That's when he heard his wife's van coming around the curve on her way back from the store. And she saw him in her headlights in the middle of the street.

It wasn't until they were sitting in their kitchen that Walters showed his wife the photos and told her what had happened. Whatever this had been, it was certainly phenomenal and amazing. But it also had the capacity to destroy his life and livelihood. Would you want to work with a building contractor who told the world that he'd been beamed into the air by a flying saucer that flew over his house and that only he and nobody else had seen?

Ed Walters didn't need anyone to answer that question for him. But he couldn't deny that in just a little over a minute a tiny window had opened, revealing to him an entire universe that he never knew existed. It was a small fissure in the complacent reality he had come to believe in. And it would change his life from that day forward. But for the time being, the couple did absolutely nothing about it. Frances Walters secretly hoped, she wrote in *The Gulf Breeze Sightings,* that this was a onetime occurrence and the whole thing would quietly go away.

But it wasn't that easy. Ed's experience was too profound to keep quiet about. Ed and Frances were sitting on bombshell photos that had to be made public, but which had the potential of tearing apart their lives. So Ed came up with a plan. What if he delivered the photos to the local newspaper but created a cover story that they'd been taken by someone else, who gave them to him for his advice? What if he never mentioned that he himself had seen the UFO, but attributed it to someone who wanted to remain anonymous? And what if he never mentioned that the person was caught by a blue beam and that the flying saucer was trying to abduct him? What if all those details remained secret, and only the photos were made public? That's what Ed and Frances decided to do.

This is a prototypical example of a cover-up of a UFO story. It was done with the best of intentions: not to keep the story secret but to reveal it in such a way that the lives of those who experienced it could go on without interruption. That was the plan.

Before a week had gone by, Ed Walters had concocted a story about having been given Polaroid photos of a UFO hovering over a neighborhood in Gulf Breeze, and delivered his story, set forth in a fictitious letter he purportedly received from a "Mr. X," along with the photos to the local newspaper. The editor pressed Walters about the identity of Mr. X, but staying true to his plan, Ed Walters refused to reveal it. Happily enough, Walters wrote, the editor of the *Sentinel* was more than pleased that the photos were taken on a Polaroid. Polaroid photos are harder to fake and therefore more likely to be authentic because there is no processing stage in which they can be doctored. The prints came out of the camera just as they'd been snapped, and if one had the originals, a lab could tell if they'd been tampered with. The photos ran in the paper two days later, and having done his part to alert any other witnesses who had seen what he had to come forward, Ed Walters hoped to put the matter to rest. Ed didn't realize what he'd started.

The Story Breaks

The story had its effect, at first, commercially and socially if nothing else. Walters wrote that the entire town of Gulf Breeze seemed seized by the idea of visitations from flying saucers. He heard snippets of conversations about them from workers at his job site, including his own subcontractors, and from fans at the local high school football game where his son was a member of the marching band. Ed Walters hoped the photos would bring new witnesses forward because he believed that others might have seen the craft that had tried to abduct him. If there were witnesses out there who had seen the same thing Ed Walters did, maybe the publication of the photos would bring them out of the woodwork.

Almost ironically, the appearance of the story in the paper was coincidental with the second appearance of the flying saucer. This time, Ed Walters's first indication that something strange was happening was a low but building humming sound inside his brain. It hit him as he walked into his house on the Friday afternoon after his UFO photos appeared in the local paper. It reminded him instantly of the humming sound that had reverberated inside his head while he was trapped inside the blue beam.

At first Walters tried to shake it off. Maybe it was a residual effect, he thought, something that would gradually disappear over time. But the hum didn't fade, it grew louder. Now his wife could see that something was wrong, watching in concern as the sound became so intense it caused him to double over. He fought to get control of it, even if only to assure his wife that he wasn't going crazy right in front of her.

What he didn't tell her was that the voice had started up again: a voice resonating in his consciousness just like the voice that had talked to him when he was frozen in the beam. He let the voice talk and feigned normality while his wife gathered up the kids and stopped in to see him in the office before she left for a football game at the local high school. He calmed her down, told her everything was all right, and said he'd meet her at the game. Finally, alone in the house, he went into his office and tried to look over the horizon to see if he could spot another UFO. But the coast seemed clear. Then he saw a tiny dot of light in the sky that moved toward him even as he recognized he was seeing the UFO. And all along the voice kept repeating something in his head that was unintelligible yet unmistakingly demanding. It wanted him to do something.

The voice was almost mechanical in its repetition. Then he heard a rushing of air and a voice that told him in clear English to step out into the open. He grabbed his camera, but another voice told him to put it down. Then there was a chorus of voices, some in English, some in other languages, telling him that taking photos was forbidden. All they wanted to do was to examine him, still another voice said, while the other voices—sounding almost as if they were together in a room—kept on telling him to move out into the street where he could be picked up. But Walters resisted. Something inside him rebelled at the insistence of the voices and the feeling he got that they were treating him as if he were a lab animal with no rights whatsoever. He took his camera.

From his vantage point at the front of the house he snapped off two pictures of the approaching UFO. As it came closer and demanded he step out into the street so they could bring him aboard, he took another photo. He began to argue with the voices in his head, complaining that he didn't have to do what they said and that whether they meant him harm or not wasn't the issue. He didn't have to follow their orders.

As Walters was debating with the chorus of voices telling him that he had to come aboard, he suddenly saw images of naked women flashing inside his brain. As he saw them—women of all types, shapes, colors, and sizes, he wrote—he knew that he was looking at real people, not photos. Who were these women? Were they aboard the flying saucer? Were these real-time images of the women whose voices he'd been hearing in his brain? Suddenly he got it. They were using the women to induce him to board the craft. They had to get him away from the house so the blue beam could envelop him. That's why they kept ordering him to step into the open. No way! He simply stood there, took another photo, and a final voice inside his head told him they'd be coming for him. Then the light disappeared.

What did it mean, they would be coming for him? Later that evening at the high school football game, he told his wife, Frances, what had happened. They wondered about the blue beam and what the threat of the voices implied. Would they come after him in the middle of a football stadium or would they wait until they could find him alone? Were they afraid of being seen or was their impunity such that they'd come after whomever they wanted without fear of witnesses? Whatever the threat meant, Ed Walters wrote, it changed the way he went about his day. Now he was carrying a gun.

By this time, Ed's photos in the local newspaper had drawn other witness reports, just as he'd hoped. Walters's original thinking had been correct: if he'd seen the flying saucer, others must have seen it as well. Now the newspaper was carrying reports from others who said that in the hours before Ed Walters had his sighting, they'd seen exactly the same craft. One woman even reported getting up in the middle of the night on the day before Walters's first encounter and seeing a blue beam issue from the craft she identified from the newspaper photo. She said she was afraid that the beam was trying to locate her barking dog. Still other witnesses told of UFO sightings ten years earlier that brought an apparent response from air force jets that tried to chase the object. So these things had been going on for a while, Walters realized, and on the very day he'd had his sighting there were others probably just as worried and concerned as he was. And now the story was heating up.

The Attempted Abduction

The local television stations serving Gulf Breeze were quick to jump on the UFO story after the *Sentinel* ran the Mr. X photos and followed up with witness reports. What had begun as one person reporting a sighting was now revealing itself to be a mass sighting as different witnesses went public to corroborate Mr. X. The photos of the brightly colored glowing circular object that looked like it had a crown on top and lots of windows along its sides had jogged the memories—or bolstered the courage—of other people, who stepped up to say they'd seen the same thing.

Ed Walters was afraid at first that his story would become the subject of derision and scorn on television. But, he wrote, that didn't come to pass. Maybe there were too many people reporting the sightings or maybe the photos spoke for themselves, but the newscasters, while maintaining a distance, didn't treat it as an "alien baby" story from one of the tabloids. Meanwhile, Walters, now carrying a gun in his pickup truck wherever he went, tried to return to his daily schedule. Wary that whoever was piloting the UFO would come after him, Ed kept a handgun on his nightstand and relied on his dog to warn him of any intruders on the property. And night after night he waited for the UFO to return to fulfill its threat to take him. He did not have to wait long.

On December 2, Ed Walters was awakened by the sound of a crying baby. It seemed so close that, as he yanked himself out of sleep, he believed it could have been in his very own house. But there was no baby, and he knew his neighbors didn't have babies either. Over the sound of the crying, a chorus of voices began speaking inside Ed Walters's brain. Then, he wrote, he heard the mechanical repetition of the computer voice and he knew that they were back. Just as they promised, they were returning for him, urging him to come outside where they could play the blue beam on him and take him into the ship. Maybe they wanted him to join the voices who were already there. But he wasn't going.

Ed awakened his wife and reached for the handgun that he kept beside the bed. He didn't speak, afraid that if he said anything "they" would hear him and home in on his voice. Meanwhile, he was still able to hear the voices arguing inside his head. It was as if he had tapped into an ongoing conversation between a couple—a man and wife who had been abducted—arguing about their baby, whom they couldn't quiet because it was hungry and their abductors wouldn't give them any milk. As bizarre as this conversation seemed, it was playing out in Spanish as Ed Walters was motioning to his wife to remain silent. He indicated that he was taking the gun and going to the front porch of the house for a look-see. Seeing nothing in the sky, he headed to the back of the house to make sure that their dog was all right. Ed had left the dog in the backyard, hoping her barks would alert them if the flying saucer returned.

Out on the pool deck he could see nothing, so he crawled out, noticed that the dog was lying there asleep, and looked up at the sky—where he saw a light grow from a tiny dot to almost the size of his house in an instant. They were coming after him, and the soft hum in his brain got incredibly loud. Just as the saucer loomed over him, Ed Walters darted back inside his house and slammed the door behind him. And this time there was no need to explain anything to his wife; she was watching the whole thing from the doorway. Now she was a witness, too, he wrote.

From inside the house he could see the UFO hovering overhead, then moving away from the house. When he opened the door for a better view, the UFO stopped and a voice ordered him to step out onto the deck. He refused, aloud, and grabbed his camera. Then, so sure that he wanted to take a photo and nothing else, he ran out onto the pool deck, aimed the Polaroid, forgetting for a critical moment about the blue beam, and took the shot. The flashbulb went off, giving away his position, and the UFO stopped. As he cursed his own stupidity for not realizing he'd had a flash cube in the camera, he scampered back across the deck and hurled himself through the door. The humming inside his head stopped and he could see the flying saucer climb out of sight.

As quickly as it had come, it was gone. Still shaking, Ed and Frances Walters got back into bed. The flying saucer had come for him three times and failed to get him into the craft. What would they do the next time? He would find out soon enough.

Ed had fallen into a heavy sleep when the sound of a dog's bark woke him up. He recognized it as his dog. But why did she stop barking? Taking his gun and his camera, Ed walked back to the rear of the house, raised the blinds on the back door, and, in shock, saw that there was a box-shaped four-foot-tall grayish black creature staring at him through the pane of glass in the door. Ed leaped backward and threw himself to the floor. The little creature just stared at him and did nothing. Ed and the creature looked at each other as if in a standoff, then Ed raised his gun and pointed it. But the creature's huge black eyes, which Ed could see through the helmet it was wearing, remained blank and impassive. The lack of expression inside those black pools was unnerving. Maybe it didn't know what a gun was, or maybe nothing Ed could do could possibly hurt it. Then the creature turned away and moved across the pool deck.

Now Ed got mad. This thing had come after him, had perhaps done something to his dog. He would go after it. Putting down his gun and his camera, Ed yanked open the door and ran across the pool deck after the dwarflike creature. Inside its armor box, it would have looked seriously menacing had it not been so small. But, Ed Walters wrote, he was mad, mad as hell that this thing had so terrorized him. He thought that if he could get his hands on it, he could bring it down. For a moment he wasn't thinking about the UFO and the voices inside his head that told him he would be taken. But his righteous anger was only too brief—because of what suddenly flashed out of the sky like a bolt of terror.

The creature had been bait, a trap, Walters realized the instant the blue beam caught his right leg in its grip. The dwarflike thing had been a lure to trick him out of the house, where the flying saucer had been lurking overhead in ambush. Now the beam, angled from behind the roof, had caught his leg and pinioned it to the pool deck, and Ed collapsed to the deck as well. He tried to drag his foot back, but it was held fast. Then he heard the back door slam as Frances came out to help pull him back inside. He yelled at her to get back inside, but he could see that his right leg was being pulled up into the beam, and the rest of his body along with it.

With one final effort, he reached out and grabbed the doorjamb to brace himself against the tug of the field. Peeking out from just over the roof overhang, he could see the great yawning maw of the flying saucer fifty feet over his head. The UFO's huge bottom hatch had opened wide, he believed, sucking him into it for whatever purposes the aliens had planned. As the toes of his left foot brushed against the edge of the blue light, he could feel the intense force field the craft must be generating to exert such a crushing pull on him. But he yanked his left foot away before it, too, got sucked in, leaving only the lower half of his right leg trapped.

Would the UFO rip him in two as Walters held on to the doorjamb for dear life? Would it sacrifice the very human life it was trying to abduct? As Frances held on to her husband, bracing against the doorjamb as well, her strength combined with Ed's brought the tug-of-war to a standstill. Then Ed could feel that he was slowly slipping away from the beam. His foot moved inside it, and then, abruptly, the beam was shut down, the blue light disappeared, and Walters went flying back into his house. He could see that the little alien life-form had gone into the fields behind his house and the craft had followed it. He took his Polaroid again and snapped a final photo as the UFO turned on its beam again, this time over the field. Maybe it was trying to retrieve the little alien, Walters wrote. As he took his picture, the blue beam was shut off, and the craft suddenly disappeared into the night sky.

Tracking the UFOs and Pursuing the Investigation

As the sightings continued through the rest of December, Walters realized that he was seeing more than one type of flying saucer. And when he heard voices inside his brain, he could differentiate between a male and a female. The voices continued to contact Ed Walters, to coax him out of his house and demand that he step into the beam and be taken aboard. It seemed to Walters that there was almost something personal about the way he was being pursued. He remembered hearing a voice saying "Zehass" over and over again to him. He speculated that maybe they had named him. Was he some sort of a pet, he asked himself in *Gulf Breeze Sightings,* or did the word have some other significance? Maybe it was the aliens' word for a human being.

During the weeks of December and the beginning of 1988, the story kept growing as more people reported seeing the UFOs that were descending over Walters's property. Drivers in the Pensacola Bay area saw the craft, as did witnesses even fifty or sixty miles away. Local television stations began reporting sightings on their evening news as the event started to draw attention from outside Gulf Breeze. The number of other witnesses chiming in and the constant stream of new photos appearing in the *Sentinel* eventually attracted the attention of MUFON, the Mutual UFO Network. Its investigators contacted the paper and reached out to Ed Walters, begging to be put in contact with Mr. X.

The subterfuge that had worked in the early weeks after Ed decided to go public with the photos was running out of fuel. Sooner or later, the pressure on Walters would be too great and the truth would come out. It would soon be time for him to blow the cover story and admit that he was Mr. X. But how much should he reveal?

Other people had seen the UFO at the same times he had, so that much had been corroborated. On the other hand, the story of the blue beam, the UFO sending sounds and voices into his head, and his encounter with an alien creature who lured him out into the open for an ambush seemed too incredible for anyone to believe. If there's one way to alienate a skeptic it's to tell him a story he can't believe, because it means he must then discard everything he's come to believe about reality just to lend you any credibility at all. The logic works against you. Therefore, it's sometimes prudent to cover up the *most* fantastic aspects of an experience just to get people to believe the *less* fantastic aspects.

Ed Walters did admit that he was Mr. X, both to Duane Cook, the editor of the *Sentinel,* and to the investigators from MUFON, who had already sent some of his Polaroid photos to the Jet Propulsion Laboratory in Pasadena, California, for their analysis. Walters would later learn from one of the analysts, Dr. Robert Nathan, that his sole job in evaluating the photos was to look for hoaxes. And even though he could not discount the possibility of extraterrestrial life among the millions of planets in the universe, he would not comment on the likelihood of extraterrestrials. He was only concerned about the validity of the photo, and his only report would be on whether or nor he had found a hoax. He would not comment upon the truth or veracity of the photos or say that this was really a photo of a flying saucer. Dr. Nathan said he would stay within the very narrow confines of what he was asked to do: find a hoax. And he would be very aggressive in looking for any such evidence.

Meanwhile, the MUFON investigators went to Ed's house with the editor of the *Sentinel* to look over the areas where Walters had spotted the UFO and to look at additional photos. They promised to keep his identity secret, but added that other people were now coming forward with their own photos. Ed still hadn't told anyone about the blue beam, the voices from the craft, or the appearance of the little creature. At the same time, the sightings and encounters had taken a strange new twist. Now, in addition to the blue beam the UFO had fired at him, they were also firing a blinding white light, just like a strobe, that flashed into his brain and caused him to have blackouts. When he woke up he'd have the strange sensation that a period of time was missing from his consciousness. This was a phenomenon he would only come to understand at a later date. At present it was still a complete mystery. And he still didn't know who or what was a "Zehass."

UFO Ambush

In one of the most frightening encounters with a UFO and the small creatures that apparently did its bidding, Walters described an early evening sighting that took place on an open road as he was driving back to a job site to check on an electrical power installation. Ed was still carrying around his shotgun in his pickup, but after a number of sightings in which he'd successfully resisted the blue beam and the telepathic orders, he decided not to live his life in fear.

On this particular evening, he was cursing at himself for not making sure that the power supply was ready for hookup on Monday morning. That was when the first flash hit him and he felt his muscles go numb and his hands lose control of the steering wheel. This was dangerous. He writes that he was traveling at high speed along the highway and was just barely able to keep control of the truck. *Bam!* Another white flash exploded in his brain as a UFO buzzed him and hovered directly overhead. He tried to get off the road so he wouldn't crash, but the UFO stayed with him and finally planted itself directly in his path.

Walters tried to slow down, but his feet, he says, had gone to rubber and he couldn't control the brakes quickly enough to avoid colliding with the UFO. So he pulled the truck off the road. He wanted to get into reverse, but his legs were barely working. His only thoughts were of the camera that had slid off the front seat onto the floor of the cab, and the shotgun behind his seat. Although he had no feeling in his hands, he turned around so that he could reach the shotgun, and managed to hook his fingers around the stock and pull it onto his lap. Then as another flash went off and threatened to knock him out completely, he rolled out of the driver's-side door and under the truck with his shotgun and camera in hand, where he positioned himself should they come after him.

The UFO hovered in place, commanding him with a voice in his head to move toward the craft because he was in real danger. Then, in a burst of blue beams, it seemed to deposit a number of the small creatures onto the road. They started moving toward him like miniature robots, clearly intent on taking him by force.

Walters said that his only thought was to pump enough energy into his muscles to allow him to get out from under the truck, slip behind the wheel, and drive home as fast as possible. He snapped off a Polaroid shot of the craft hovering above the road, and then, because the little creatures were moving so slowly and sensation was returning to his limbs, he was able to roll out from under the truck and climb back into the driver's seat before the blue beam could immobilize him. He was still weak, but he had feeling in his hands. He put the truck into reverse, backed off the shoulder, and gunned it all the way across the road. Then he turned the truck around, and with the little control he had over his hands, he steered toward the main highway as far away from the flying saucer as he could get. When the saucer was out of sight and he was sure it wasn't following him, he pulled over again onto the shoulder and waited until full sensation came back into his limbs before he ventured out into highway traffic. Then he drove home as fast as he could.

He'd been ambushed on an open road, but he'd escaped. A small platoon of little creatures had come after him, but he'd gotten away. His story was out in the open now, but he knew that he couldn't cover up the attempted abductions much longer. Things were coming to a crisis, and at some point he would have to go public with every detail. Life as he had lived it was quickly coming to an end. He just wished he understood one thing: why him?

The Expert Investigators

MUFON area director Donald Ware and the other investigators from MUFON, although impressed by the Polaroid photos and Ed's account, sought what for them would be even more definitive corroboration from an independent source that the photographs taken by Ed Walters were real and not creations. Analysts at JPL had already reported that they could find no evidence of hoaxes in the processing of the photos, but there were still more questions to answer. Donald Ware and his colleagues contacted Walt Andrus, the head of MUFON, and asked him to conduct a personal interview. Accordingly, in January 1988, Andrus, the founder of MUFON and one of the more respected figures in UFO investigations, came to Gulf Breeze to meet Walters and see the photos and the ongoing investigation firsthand.

Andrus wrote a report in which he personally vouched

for the authenticity of the Walters photos and of Ed Walters himself. Interestingly, Andrus laid the groundwork for a lot of the arguments in favor of Ed Walters's honesty when he said that for a person with such an obvious stake in his own credibility to embark on a hoax of this magnitude would be nothing short of self-destructive. Because he was a building contractor and a member of community planning committees, Ed Walters could not afford to become a subject of derision. Therefore, his disclosure of the information about the UFOs he photographed, which would expose him to ridicule, was serious because of the impact on his own life. That decision, combined with the kinds of photos he saw, led the director of MUFON to pronounce that this was no hoax—and probably one of the most intriguing series of UFO encounters anyone had ever witnessed.

In February 1988, to continue the investigation under a more controlled set of circumstances, MUFON provided Ed Walters with a four-lens Nimslo preloaded camera in which the film was sealed inside to prevent tampering. The special aspect of this camera was its ability to expose four frames at a single time through separate lenses. This enabled the camera to expose four nearly identical frames at the same time, providing photo analysts with different exact originals of the same shot. They didn't have to destroy a negative in order to analyze it. They also exposed one image in advance so that the film was already lined up on the sprockets. Any attempt to remove the film and reload it could be detected by examining the sprockets that advanced the film.

Then, U.S. Navy consultant and physicist Dr. Bruce Maccabee suggested that Ed Walters create a special stereoscopic camera arrangement in which two identical Polaroid cameras were mounted a fixed distance apart on a two-foot board, which itself was mounted onto a tripod with a common shutter connecting the cameras. This, Dr. Maccabee suggested, would provide a more accurate measurement of distance and size by exposing two frames at exactly the same time and with a premeasured distance between the lenses. By knowing how far apart the lenses were at the exact moment of exposure, analysts should be better able to determine more about the dimensions of the objects Ed Walters was photographing.

Also in February, at the suggestion of the investigators, Ed Walters submitted to a polygraph test in which he was asked straight-out whether he was lying about the UFOs or trying to be deceptive about them in any way. By this time, Walters had revealed to the investigators that he had not only seen the UFOs, but been pursued by them, trapped more than once in a blue beam that was supposed to bring him into the craft, and advanced upon by small creatures who were sent to capture him. The polygraph operator asked him specifically about these experiences and said in his March 1988 report that he could find no evidence of any consistent deception in Walters's test. In other words, the polygraph operator wrote, Ed Walters believed that what he was telling the investigators was the truth.

The Controversy

The strange visitors in business suits were unnerving, Frances Walters wrote in her section of *The Gulf Breeze*

Sightings. She first saw them through the front window, conservatively dressed men who were obviously surveilling the house and walking up to her front porch to see if anyone was home. Frances avoided them completely and hid behind doorways until they left. Then Ed Walters himself was visited. The strangers identified themselves as U.S. Air Force intelligence personnel, then slapped him with a materials warrant for the original photos that had run in the *Sentinel*. Walters told them he didn't have them and sent them on their way; the photos had been turned over to MUFON for analysis. Clearly, however, important people were taking a serious interest in what was turning up in the paper. It might have started out as an oddball human interest story, but the military seemed to have recognized that when a lot of people start reporting the same kinds of objects flying through the sky at the same time near a vital U.S. nuclear warfare facility, something might just be up there.

Requests to the military to run an investigation into the sightings were met with official derision. Radar readings from military installations around the area, air force and navy spokespersons said, didn't register any strange craft in the area. And although the military was checking out the story, they didn't perceive the UFOs as a threat—or so the public information officers said. Per official government policy, even if senior officers at the naval air station were sitting in front of military radars biting their nails at the intrusions they couldn't prevent, they could not admit to it.

Over the course of the next two months, a unit from one of the air defense commands would erect low-altitude radar tracking stations, and the army would test a radar blimp that hovered over Pensacola Bay. The blimp quickly became a symbol to the Gulf Breeze community. In the face of the navy's and air force's strenuous denials of any unusual activity in this most sensitive of air corridors, the blimp was a striking example of the army's response to what was obviously perceived by the area military command as a threat. Meanwhile, spokesmen from the army, navy, and air force steadfastly maintained they had no information about UFO sightings in the area.

Almost immediately after the initial publicity on the sightings, some critics claimed that Gulf Breeze was a "community hoax" perpetrated on the rest of the country. The witnesses who stepped forward to corroborate one another's stories were all part of a coordinated plan to create a tourist attraction in Gulf Breeze, the critics said. And for a while the town did become the site of a pilgrimage made by ufologists to see what they could in the nighttime sky and talk to witnesses.

Other debunkers popped up to claim that the photos were faked. Experts showed how they were able to superimpose a model of a flying disk onto existing photos of famous buildings and make them look real. Some even claimed that they could use a Polaroid camera and a pie tin to create the same images in the Walters photos and suggested the entire event was concocted to make heroes out of the locals and to sell books and make movies.

One of the criticisms leveled at MUFON investigators was their lack of research into Ed Walters's background. Allegations were tossed back and forth about a possible Ed Walters police record for joy riding in a stolen car. Other stories involved rumors of financial irregularities. Should these stories have been checked out, investigators asked, prior to MUFON's involvement in the case? Other researchers and supporters of Ed and Frances Walters said that any previous run-ins with the law were irrelevant as far as the photos were concerned; either the photos held up to analysis or they didn't, a person's background made no difference when evaluating the physical evidence of a photograph. When Ed's photos passed the initial test, it was all the MUFON investigators needed to take the investigation to the next stages.

As if all the criticism weren't enough, Walters said about the six-month period of the sightings, people around town were learning his identity and that he was the person who had had the UFO experiences. Now he was being phoned directly by other people who had claimed to have UFO encounters. He was also called in on interviews with people who were trying to hoax their own experiences to mimic his own. Were these people doing it for profit or was there an organized debunking operation under way to set Ed Walters up for public humiliation? Even Bruce Maccabee had tried to test Walters's veracity by taking a phony photograph of a model that he'd set up on a stretch of road where Walters had had a sighting and asking him whether it was a UFO that he recognized. Walters said that it wasn't. But when he realized that he had been set up by someone he'd been working with—even though, as he wrote later, he understood the need for the verification—he was stung. It was no wonder, Walters realized, that many people were reluctant to come forward with UFO experiences. You turn yourself into a public commodity in which anyone who claims to be an investigator can demand you go to great lengths to get their endorsement of your story.

Rex Salisberry, a onetime leader of the MUFON investigation into the Gulf Breeze sightings, was quoted in *UFO Magazine* back in 1992 that according to photo analyst William Hyzer, in an article he published in *Photo Methods* magazine, some of the Ed Walters Polaroid photos were faked. Salisberry also referred to stories about models of UFOs that were used to create some of the photos and how Walters was alleged to have enlisted the aid of a family friend to help him suspend models of UFOs from wires in order to rig the photos. Even people in the Gulf Breeze/Pensacola areas, according to Salisberry, believed that much of the entire sightings incidents were setups, but that because the Gulf Breeze sights were really a mixture of a number of incidents, each one should have its own separate investigation.

The "model UFO" story provided Gulf Breeze supporters and debunkers alike with ammunition for their respective arguments. It began with the seemingly fortuitous discovery of a paper model that newspapers claimed was the object Walters used in his photographs. A reporter—whom Walters believes had to have been tipped off by a source—showed up at a house Walters had built and asked the owners whether they had ever seen a small model of a UFO. When the owners showed them something they'd discovered shortly after they'd moved in, it became a newspaper headline: GULF BREEZE UFO MODEL FOUND.

Walters refuted the charge. Not only was the model the wrong size for the photo, because it was too big for the background, it was the wrong shape and therefore couldn't have been the object that turned up in the enlarged photos. The model had been fabricated from a set of Walters's building plans dated 1989, over a year after Walters had shot the first set of photographs. Others, however, said that Walters's explanation was a complete fabrication to cover up the discovery of the model he used to stage the UFO appearance. Who's telling the truth?

What's fascinating about the model story and the possible attempts to use chicanery to debunk the Gulf Breeze story is that it correlates with the CIA's own practice of publicly discrediting anyone who came forward with a UFO story to tell. Could it be that the CIA has a circle of favored reporters who are tipped off to debunking "scoops" in advance?

The Abductions

One of the investigators who was contacted by MUFON and who was intrigued by the descriptions in the *Sentinel* was the renowned alien abduction researcher and author Budd Hopkins. In his book, *Missing Time,* Hopkins helped explain the phenomenon in which people report bizarre disorienting experiences with respect to UFO sightings and encounters in which there are periods of time they can't account for. Ever since the publicity surrounding the experience of Barney and Betty Hill, who were one of the first couples ever to talk about having been abducted by a UFO, researchers have sought a scientific, measurable basis behind the highly subjective stories of individuals from whose lives chunks of time are simply gone. By working with hypnotic memory regression to help people recover memories of that missing time, Hopkins is among a group of therapists, including

Dr. Jonathan Mack at Harvard, who have sought to put some rational explanation into place for what happens to people who claim to have been abducted.

Ed Walters turned to Budd Hopkins and clinical psychologist Dr. Dan C. Overlade at a critical time during the publicity that surrounded him when the accusations of fraud and duplicity had threatened to overwhelm the entire story. It didn't matter that during the first few months of 1988, when the sightings continued, anybody could have gone down to Gulf Breeze to confirm Ed Walters's story. It didn't matter that photo experts had declared that the Polaroids Walters took were no hoax. Walters had said he'd seen a flying saucer and that was akin to blasphemy. Ed Walters became the central figure of public controversy even as the fear of the aliens and why they wanted him kept eating away at his psyche.

In seeking answers to the mysterious relationship he seemed to have with the entities that beamed the voices into his head and kept calling him "Zehass," he sought help from Dan Overlade, who began a series of therapy sessions. Now, in 1988, Walters began another journey, this one backward in time, where he discovered that he'd experienced alien abductions for years prior to his conscious memories of seeing his first UFO. How could these memories have been erased as if the abductions had never occurred?

Bit by bit, he and Overlade pieced together what happened to him. Some of these images were horrifying. From deep within a regressive state, he described having been held down with great force by creatures who kept ordering him to stop moving. He relived the moment, screaming out as, in his mind, he tried to resist.

But not only were the creatures too strong, they were able to paralyze him with a white beam that shot out like a flash, freezing his muscles and rendering him incapable of any further resistance. In successive therapy sessions, Walters began to realize that he had been the subject of alien experiments and visitations going all the way back to his twenties. He realized that his faulty memories of incidents in which he couldn't account for sudden jumps in time, or falling asleep in one spot and waking up in another, made perfect sense when the pieces of what happened to him during an abduction were fitted back into place. If there were questions in his mind about why the aliens piloting the UFO selected him, they were resolved by his discovery of his long association with the abduction phenomenon. Ed Walters was a subject of alien experimentation, or at least that's what he came to believe as a result of psychological investigations with his therapist.

The Sightings Continue

When the publicity is over after a high-profile event such as the Gulf Breeze sightings, few reporters ever follow the continuing story. In Gulf Breeze, as in Phoenix ten years later, the sightings continued well after the hubbub died away. In 1990, for example, MUFON investigators Anne and Bruce Morrison were drawn back to the Gulf Breeze story by renewed reports of UFOs in the skies over Pensacola Bay. They believed that since so many people were watching the skies and reporting having seen objects, maybe they'd be lucky enough to have their own sighting. And over the course of the next year, they were joined by upward of seventy-five people at nighttime watches that resulted in the recording of over a hundred sightings.

Capturing on video and still cameras images of hanging red lights in the sky, larger white balls of light, and a strange pulsating red light—none of which made any sound as they moved through the air—witnesses were amazed at the mobility of what seemed to them to be unidentified aircraft of some sort. Even military and civilian pilots and flight controllers joined the group watching the Gulf Breeze skies during 1990 and 1991 and were similarly impressed with the strange nature of the lights. Even the military personnel present confirmed that these were not any military aircraft that they could identify, and certainly not flares or incendiary devices or any kind of craft that they were familiar with.

The lights, according to Art Hufford in *UFO Magazine,* weren't simply floating across the sky, they were engaged in a complex series of aerial maneuvers, doing barrel rolls, flipping from a "vertical to a horizontal orientation," and blocking out the night sky between them. This, according to some observers, led people to believe that the lights were attached to a larger object. The lights seemed to move under their own control and were not affected by air currents, seemingly eliminating the possibility of flares suspended from parachutes. Were these the same lights that Ed Walters photographed? Some observers said no, especially since the lights seemed attached to one another. Could these sightings have been another example of the kinds of objects that floated over Phoenix in 1997?

Other witnesses reported seeing and photographing lights that formed part of a disk. These lights outlined the shape of a large disk reminiscent of the UFO that Ed Walters first saw four years earlier. This time, however, instead of a blue-gray glow or a series of orange lights, the witnesses saw only red lights hovering in the sky over Gulf Breeze High School.

The sightings continued through the end of 1991, diminishing in intensity and frequency. When they disappeared for a while only the questions remained. How much of what Ed Walters said he saw was true and how much was either an embellishment or a confabulation? Did, as Rex Salisberry asked in *UFO Magazine,* the investigators from MUFON and elsewhere ask the right questions and look for discrepancies in the stories? Did Walters's stories of abductions and the attempts to levitate him conform to a preexisting model of what these stories were supposed to sound like so as to attract the interest of abduction investigators? And for what possible reason would Ed Walters call such attention to himself and his family? There are very few answers.

Beyond the photos themselves, much of the Gulf Breeze story relies on the personal narrative of Ed Walters. His photos of Frances running frantically away from a blue beam that shoots into the frame of one of the photos is compelling and dramatic. But it is the sketch of the little alien creature and the reptile who appeared as part of his recovered memory therapy that also force us to ask whether there are certain people who live a double life. They are residents of this reality on planet Earth, going through their days confident that the basic premises of their lives are true. Yet, at the same time, they might be the subjects of bizarre experiments performed on them by alien creatures. Abducted from their bedrooms or from behind the wheels of their cars, portions of their memories are simply excised by these creatures and are recovered only as a result of extensive therapy. Who's to say where the truth is?

Perhaps complicated UFO stories such as Gulf Breeze are the result of real events, delusions, or out-and-out embellishments. The debunkers seize on the embellishments, others seize on the delusions, but the real researchers who find clear and convincing evidence of an unknown presence are often drowned out in the noise. Remember, the CIA has said that it is government policy not only to deny the presence of UFOs and any government interest in them, but to discredit as much as possible those people involved in any UFO belief system. That in itself should be a caveat to anyone following the ongoing story of the Gulf Breeze sightings and the narrative of those who experienced them.

CHAPTER 5

The UFO Encounters at Bentwaters

> *"Of course flying saucers are real—and they are interplanetary."*
>
> Air Chief Marshall Lord Dowling, head of
> the Royal Air Force during World War II, 1954

AMONG THE MANY STORIES OF MILITARY ENCOUNTERS with UFOs are some amazing descriptions of alien spacecraft landing at secure military bases, where they meet with top military and political leaders. President Truman was purported to have met with a delegation of aliens after the shootdown of a spacecraft over Roswell in 1947, beginning a long-term U.S. cooperation with extraterrestrials not to challenge them militarily and to keep their presence on Earth a secret. In return, the United States was said to have reaped a harvest of technology that blossomed into commercial and consumer products as well as military weapons from the 1960s through the present.

President Eisenhower was also purported to have met with aliens in 1954 at Edwards Air Force Base, where he looked over their spacecraft and listened to a proposal from the extraterrestrials that they be allowed to make their presence known to humanity. The result, they supposedly promised Eisenhower, was a new age of enlightenment for humanity in which they'd come to understand their relationship to life in the universe.

"We're not ready," President Eisenhower was said to have answered, according to the Earl of Clancarty, who quoted a RAF pilot present at the meeting. All the witnesses to this meeting have long since died, so there are no individuals now living who can give firsthand testimony as to whether this conversation actually took place. But people who said they were present did comment, as reported in an article by Brad Steiger in *Unsolved UFO Sightings Magazine* (Vol. 5, no. 4 [1998]). Eisenhower explained to the extraterrestrials that any announcement of their presence on Earth would throw human populations into a panic. It would completely overthrow the institutions of government and result in widespread destruction.

The aliens would accede to the president's wishes, at least for the present, they told him. Their greater mission was still to bring humanity into the community of other civilizations, but they understood how their announced presence could create havoc rather than result in benefits. They told Eisenhower that they would remain a presence on Earth, however, contacting individual human beings and establishing their own facilities so as to educate humanity and prepare them through selected disclosure for the day when they would reveal their presence. Eisenhower agreed to cooperate and the deal was struck. The aliens would remain, make contact with individuals, study humanity, and help a select group of humans prepare the rest of the planet for a full disclosure. The world's governments would not interfere, but would study the aliens in turn, and the aliens would share their technology with humanity.

As exciting as these stories may be, they are little more than rumor. Even though the now famous MJ12 papers seem to document some of the government's top secret study of alien spacecraft and their inhabitants since the 1947 Roswell crash, there is ongoing debate about the veracity of the MJ12 documents as well. Therefore, when a story comes along about a UFO encounter at a military facility that is apparently backed up by an official memo from a senior air force officer and released from military sources, that story tends to stand out from the rest of the pack.

Moreover, when the story is backed up by multiple eyewitnesses—civilian as well as military—a tape recording of the event, and a furious attempt by military authorities to cover it up, one should suspect that there is some truth to the narrative. This accumulation of evidence includes a written memo released by the air force and eyewitness accounts describing what happened in 1980 at Bentwaters, a joint RAF/U.S. Air Force critical NATO air base in the English countryside near the North Sea.

It was the second time a UFO story had become associated with RAF Bentwaters and Woodbridge. Buried deep within the files of the U.S. National Security Agency are reports of UFO sightings at Bentwaters, both visual and on radar, that took place in the 1950s. The stories of these sightings might have quietly faded into obscurity (only to be resurrected by the COMETA report in 1998) had it not been for another startling series of visitations in 1980. This time, however, because of multiple witnesses and television reports, the RAF Bentwaters case would become Britain's most important UFO sighting, rivaling the crash at Roswell in the United States.

The Memo

On January 13, 1981, U.S. Air Force Lieutenant Colonel Charles I. Halt, the deputy base commander at Bentwaters, wrote a memo on official air force letterhead to describe the incidents of "unexplained lights" that took place in December 1980. The memo, now declassified and released by the USAF under the Freedom of Information Act, reads:

1. Early in the morning of 27 Dec 80 (approximately 0300L), two USAF security police patrolmen saw unusual lights outside the back gate at RAF Woodbridge. Thinking an aircraft might have crashed or been forced down, they called for permission to go outside the gate to investigate. The on-duty flight chief responded and allowed three patrolmen to proceed on foot. The individuals reported seeing a strange glowing object in the forest. The object was described as being metallic in appearance and triangular in shape, approximately two to three meters across the base and approximately two meters high. It illuminated the entire

forest with a white light. The object itself had a pulsing red light on top and a bank(s) of blue lights underneath. The object was hovering on legs. As the patrolmen approached the object, it maneuvered through the trees and disappeared. At this time the animals on a nearby farm went into a frenzy. The object was briefly sighted approximately an hour later near the back gate.

2. The next day, three depressions 1½" deep and 7" in diameter were found where the object had been sighted on the ground. The following night (29 Dec 80) the area was checked for radiation. Beta/gamma readings of 0.1 milliroentgens were recorded with peak readings in the three depressions and near the center of the triangle formed by the depressions. A nearby tree had moderate (.05–.07) readings on the side of the tree toward the depressions.

3. Later in the night a red sun-like light was seen through the trees. It moved and pulsed. At one point it appeared to throw off glowing particles and then broke into five separate white objects and then disappeared. Immediately thereafter, three star-like objects were noticed in the sky, two objects to the north and one to the south, all of which were about 10° off the horizon. The objects moved rapidly in sharp angular movements and displayed red, green and blue lights. The objects to the north appeared to be elliptical through an 8–12 power lens. They then turned to full circles. The objects to the north remained in the sky for an

hour or more. The object to the south was visible for two or three hours and beamed down a stream of light from time to time. Numerous individuals, including the undersigned, witnessed the activities in paragraphs 2 and 3.

(signed)

Charles I. Halt, Lt. Col, USAF
Deputy Base Commander

This is an absolutely stunning memo. Although it doesn't describe the appearances of alien life-forms and their communication with military officers, it nonetheless appears to document a series of UFO sightings on a tightly secured NATO base. While skeptics have said that air force personnel claiming to have seen strange lights in the forest were, in reality, looking at the beacon from a nearby lighthouse, no one has really stepped forward to debunk the memo as either disinformation or a hoax. And what would be Lieutenant Colonel Halt's purpose in writing a hoax memo? After the Bentwaters incident, Charles Halt was promoted and named commander of the Bentwaters complex. The powers that be in the U.S. Air Force command hierarchy deemed that Colonel Halt had done his job well and rewarded him with a promotion and his own command.

Lieutenant Colonel Halt's memo was part of a file on Bentwaters that has become a holy grail for UFO researchers since stories about the lights at Bentwaters first began circulating in the UK and the U.S. The official file has never been fully disclosed. Only the Halt memo itself was eventually made public by the British—after

U.S. Air Force authorities had denied its existence. Even though a number of air force personnel have gone public about their encounters with the lights in Rendlesham Forest, the air force itself has continued to deny that anything out of the ordinary took place in the days after Christmas, 1980. But, bit by bit, pieced together from eyewitness accounts, the story of what happened is finally taking shape.

The first indications that unusual events had taken place around the Bentwaters Air Force Base came from stories told by local residents of the Rendlesham Forest area that they had seen strange lights overhead around Christmas, 1980. The people who lived in the rural district were more than used to the comings and goings of NATO jets in the area. But the lights they saw over the forest were different. They weren't accompanied by the thundering roar of jet engines or the *thwap thwap* of helicopter rotors, all too common sounds in the overhead air corridors used by military aircraft. Also, even though the residents along this part of the southern coast of the North Sea were used to seeing pieces of Soviet launch vehicles burn up in the atmosphere, these lights didn't seem to look like falling debris. Nor did they resemble shooting stars or meteors burning up in the atmosphere. People walking their dogs in the early-morning hours of December 26, 1980, reported lights behaving nothing like falling objects.

Objects were also tracked coming over the North Sea coast by an array of military and civilian flight control radars. But because it was the Christmas holiday, air traffic was light and the objects were at first assumed to be debris from a falling Soviet Cosmos satellite that had been traveling on a northwest course from southern Europe over the North Sea.

In her 1998 study of the Bentwaters case, *UFO Crash Landing?*, researcher Jenny Randles suggested that highly advanced surveillance and analysis systems, perhaps used by extraterrestrials, could determine in advance what course space vehicles might take upon reentering Earth's atmosphere and use the radar blips from those falling objects to mask their own intrusions into protected airspaces. (This is not at all far-fetched; during the 1960s and 1970s, highly classified U.S. test aircraft often hid within the radar signatures of commercial jets flying over Nevada so as to mask themselves from radar detection. A lot of these mysterious aircraft lights were reported as UFOs by civilian observers and even commercial pilots.)

Eyewitnesses Describe the Incident

It was the strange array of colored lights gradually descending from the sky that first attracted the attention of the two USAF Air Police. They watched as the lights overhead disappeared into the thickest part of Rendlesham Forest. The men were on patrol at around two in the morning, December 26, 1980. One of them looked into the forest, saw the lights, and asked his partner if he'd ever seen anything like that before. The two of them just stared for a minute at the light show ahead of them. Could it be the flickering flames from a downed aircraft?

The Air Police unit drove across the perimeter, leaving the base grounds by the east gate, and headed into the woods for a better view of whatever was causing the lights. But the closer they got, the stranger the thing looked. It certainly was not a downed aircraft; they found no sign of debris nor any track of a crippled airplane smashing its way to destruction. The light source seemed to be sitting on the ground or hovering barely above it, though the scene was obscured by the thick pine forest.

Finally, one of the Air Police got out of the truck. Negotiating the narrow forestry road, he headed right to the edge of the thick branches to get a better look at the object. But as he did so, the object, eerily glowing in colors like a decorated Christmas tree, gradually changed to become more intensely white. He could feel an increase in the tension around him as if he had walked to the edge of a force field. It was physical, palpable; even the density of the air seemed to change. This sensation sent the frightened airman fleeing back to his truck and his partner, and the two drove back onto the base and turned in a report to the desk sergeant.

The more the two airmen talked to their sergeant over the base phone, the more all of them realized that this was not really a police matter at all. Whatever was out there in the forest had nothing to do with the commission of a crime or with base personnel violating one of the rules. The desk sergeant was resistant to doing anything about the lights. If the incident had been a plane crash, he had a set procedure to follow. But this wasn't a plane crash, it was more of a base security issue. So the sergeant connected the two airmen through to Central Security Control. He'd let the higher-ups make a determination about what the two airmen saw.

Central Security

If the desk sergeant seemed unconcerned with the report from the two Air Police patrolmen, the dispatcher at Central Security seemed alarmed. "Stay right where you are," he ordered the two police officers. "I'm dispatching a unit to your position."

When the USAF sergeant from CSC arrived, he directed the police officers to show him what they saw. They pointed to the glow just through the forest on the other side of the gate. The sergeant, James Penniston, could see the lights now, but they looked to him like the residual burning that he'd seen at many crash sites. Whatever went down in the forest, he thought, looked as though it had been burning for a while. He asked the two Air Police if they'd seen the plane crash or heard the sound of a plane going down. Did they hear any sounds at all?

But the two just shook their heads and told the security sergeant that this wasn't a crash. Whatever had come out of the sky had simply landed and was just sitting there. They hadn't approached the object because of the odd sensation in the air when they'd started to get close. They'd only seen the glowing lights through the trees when they entered the forest. And then the glowing lights changed color. As soon as they saw it change color and felt the heaviness in the air, they drove back to base to report it. So Sergeant Penniston phoned in what he considered to be a plane crash report, of possibly an A-10, possibly something else, to Security Control.

Security checked with the control tower, who told

them there were no planes in the air that night. Penniston walked back to the east gate to stare at the glow again, and the two Air Police repeated their story that this was no crash. They hadn't seen a plane go down and only noticed flashing lights overhead which entered the forest. Then they saw the brightly lit object, at least they thought it was an object, glowing at them through the trees. It was just suddenly there, as if it had landed. But it certainly didn't crash.

They'd have to take a closer look, Penniston realized, and do some investigating for a report. That meant leaving the base again and getting as close to the object as they could. But it didn't require all of them to trek into the woods. Penniston took one of the airmen with him. They retraced the same route that the airmen had originally taken, back toward the edge of the woods and onto the dirt forestry road that should lead directly to the crash site. They planned to stay in radio contact with the base, making sure that when they found the object they could quickly call for help.

But things changed dramatically as Sergeant Penniston and his small unit drove deeper into the forest. First the radio transmissions began to break up. That made no sense. It was a clear night with no other traffic around and nothing flying around overhead that could interfere with reception, or so they thought. Maybe it was the denseness of the forest. So Penniston ordered his driver to stop and get out of the vehicle. He would maintain a straight-line radio relay with the base while Penniston tried to get closer to the lights. They would try to keep him in sight, and he would forward their transmissions back to the base. It was a cold night, but the driver would have to stand outside nevertheless while Penniston and the original police officer went deeper into the forest on foot.

As they moved up to the tree line Penniston seemed more convinced than ever he was looking at the wreckage from a plane crash. The way the lights moved reminded him of a fuel residue fire burning itself out. But such a fire should have ignited some of the foliage, and he should feel the heat from a fuel and wood fire even at that distance. Moreover, there was no odor of burning jet fuel or smoldering wood. Perhaps it was the freezing temperatures and the direction of the wind that prevented him from smelling anything or feeling the heat. He crept closer, along with the Air Police officer, until the radio transmissions almost cut out again. This time, not only were they having a problem hearing transmissions between the driver and the base, the communication signal between Penniston and his driver was breaking up. What kind of disturbance could be interfering with their radios? Maybe he should establish another relay point, the base security sergeant thought, and ordered the Air Police officer to take up position at the very edge of the forest while he moved a hundred or so feet forward to get a closer look at the lights.

As he got closer, the lights began to change color, and suddenly what looked like the flicker from flames now had a shape and wasn't really flickering at all. When Penniston saw what was sitting out there in the clearing he realized that he wasn't looking at the flaming wreck of an A-10 at all, but something very different.

It was at almost that same moment that the airman Penniston had left at the perimeter decided that he was not going to be out there all alone, not now, on a sub-freezing night in the middle of a forest with the strangest thing he'd ever seen in his life changing colors through the trees. So he got a move on and caught up with Penniston, who was by now coming up on the area where the object was sitting.

Through the pine branches, Penniston could see that the array of glowing lights was sitting amid a small clearing just ahead of him. All but obscured by the forest that surrounded it, the clearing stood at the end of the narrow forestry track. Unless you knew the forest you wouldn't even be aware of the clearing at night, except, now, for the strange colored lights that seemed to be dancing on the other side of the trees.

As the two men approached the clearing, it was apparent that they were staring at a brightly lit object, not a meteor, not a flaming airplane fuselage, but something that had a definite shape and, terrifyingly, seemed to be aware of their presence. It changed color and began to glow very bright, and the men, not knowing what to think, hit the dirt as if it were going to fire a weapon at them. Maybe it was a scene from *War of the Worlds,* but the two air force enlisted men were taking no chances. They saw what they later said was a vaguely triangular-shaped object that had a kind of opaque surface illuminated from within. It was the size of a large military vehicle, maybe a tank, but it was clearly not a familiar shape.

Still facedown, Sergeant Penniston realized that he'd have to make some kind of report, so he got to his feet and motioned for the other airman to accompany him for a closer look. The object now seemed to be standing or suspended just a foot or so off the ground. If it were supported by landing gear or struts, the supports were obscured by the object's brilliant glow, and this made the object seem even more strange. Nevertheless, the airmen crept closer and began to notice that their movements were becoming more labored as they were making their way through heavier air.

As if an invisible field of energy were closing in around them, the men began to feel the effects of some kind of electrical disturbance on their bodies. Their hair began to stand up as if it were electrostatically charged. They seemed to move slower, and it was difficult to take footsteps the closer they got. Was the object generating some kind of defensive field that prevented intruders from getting too close? Were they enveloped in some kind of electronic energy field? It sure felt that way. Worse, it felt as if space and time themselves around the object were somehow bent and distorted. Maybe the object had the power to so distort physical reality that humans, animals, or anything that got close experienced a kind of system shutdown. Whatever it was, Penniston felt like he was swimming upstream through quicksand to reach the object.

The security control officer, whose interview appears in the Jenny Randles book *UFO Crash Landing?*, said that by the time he was only a few feet away from the object, he could see that its glasslike surface had a series of symbols or markings on it as if they'd been etched into the surface. They struck him as oddly familiar, but he couldn't figure out where he could have seen anything like them before. The two airmen stayed with the object, inspecting it from the closest vantage point they could reach, until the thing took off.

First it seemed to retract landing gear that was now visible. It hadn't been hovering at all, but resting on three short struts or legs hidden by the white glow. The craft—they now realized it was indeed a craft—pulled the struts back into its body and suddenly rose a few feet from the forest floor. Then it seemed to glide through the trees without a sound, deftly avoiding the branches and limbs as it moved backward away from them and then hung in the air just above the treetops. Then, in what seemed like an instant, it was gone, soaring straight into the air. What struck the two men the most was that there was not even a hint of acceleration. It was almost as though the object were able to reverse gravity, levitating instead of blasting off, lifting off the ground so effortlessly it was clear that it demonstrated a technology neither man had ever seen before.

In the absence of the object, whatever power the force field held over the men suddenly collapsed and there was a brief moment of absolute chilling silence. Then, like air rushing in to fill a vacuum, the chattering night sounds of a normal forest poured into the silence and the world as the airmen knew it was alive once again. But what had they really seen? Had they actually stumbled across a real UFO, not a dream, not a practical joke, not some mystery military aircraft that either the RAF or the USAF was testing on Christmas Day because they figured they'd have no witnesses? In that return to reality, when life flooded back into the forest, the security sergeant and the air patrolman simply didn't know.

What they also didn't know was that things back at the base were becoming critical. The original call placed by the two air policemen to security about the aircraft's appearance just before it landed in the forest had been followed up. In fact, the object had been tracked by multiple radars as it came in over the North Sea. RAF Bentwaters's own radar had tracked it along with another radar command center until it dropped below their coverage in an area that would have coincided with Rendlesham Forest. Suddenly this was a security alert, made urgent by the loss of radio contact with Penniston and his unit once they entered the forest. Security Control considered them lost and mounted a search. That was when the control tower saw the object take off from the forest in a blaze of light.

The two airmen, who encountered a base security control unit when they walked out of the forest, were debriefed by a security officer. Sergeant Penniston reported they'd only seen some lights in the forest, nothing more. Maybe there were some impressions on the ground left by whatever was holding the lights, but he couldn't be sure. And whatever it was that had been there wasn't there now, he said.

The security officer told them that something had been picked up on base radar and tracked to the area where they had been looking. If they believed that something might have left an indentation on the ground, they should look for it after sunup. What the two airmen didn't know, however, as they tried not to seem like a pair of lunatics in a frenzy after a flying saucer sighting, was that an A-10 with infrared sensors had picked up a heat signature from the forest where the men had seen the object. Maybe there would be some evidence left there after all.

After sunup, when the local police had been notified about an incident that took place within their jurisdiction, Penniston returned to the site with the other airman and found exactly what they were hoping they wouldn't find: impressions left by the craft's landing gear. But there was more. Directly over the impressions was a kind of break in the thick tree canopy where the craft had ascended before it hovered at the treetops and then shot away. So not only was the landing site marked on the ground, but the actual trees contained evidence that something had been there above the ground. Now the airmen knew that what they'd seen had been no trick of the eyes.

The local police were eager to get rid of this madness, however, and quickly dismissed the impressions as animal tracks. Although Penniston disagreed and tried to get the police who met them at the site to notice the exact distances between the triangular outline of the impressions and the perfect shapes of the impressions themselves, it was useless to argue. Their minds were made up, why confuse them with facts? So the airmen stopped arguing and Colonel Ted Conrad, the base commander who had originally called the local police, didn't argue either. Let the local police run their investigation or not, he thought, he still had to push his reports up through channels and treat this matter, whatever it turned out to be, as if it were real and a possible security breach. So the United States Air Force investigation went forward, sweeping more people into a growing circle of officers and enlisted personnel who became aware of the strange goings-on in Rendlesham Forest.

By the afternoon of December 27, that circle had grown to include Lieutenant Colonel Halt, the deputy base commander, who became involved when the security control desk sergeant reported to him what Penniston and the other airman had phoned in the night before. Colonel Halt told the desk sergeant to make sure the information found its way into the official record just in case the event turned out to be related to a plane crash. He'd rather have a notation of the event somewhere than have it brought up to him later during a formal investigation.

Next, Halt conferred with his boss, base commander Colonel Conrad, who agreed that there had to be something put into the record even though neither man really thought it was an alien spacecraft. Maybe both officers thought the whole event would fade away and that it was a onetime only occurrence. But if that's what they were thinking, the events of that night would prove them dramatically wrong.

Alien Encounter

So much activity occurred in so many different places in Rendlesham Forest on the night of December 27 that it's surprising so many of the witnesses' stories coincide on the basic facts. Nevertheless, there are still major discrepancies in the stories from different parts of the forest, and major arguments among the witnesses about whether there actually were aliens present.

If you take as gospel the story told by USAF airman Larry Warren, who in his book *Left at East Gate* (written with Peter Robbins) says he was there that night and witnessed an alien encounter, then the Bentwaters case represents one of the most incredible UFO stories since 1947. If you accept the account of Colonel Charles Halt, who disputes Larry Warren and says he was never there in the forest that night, the story is still incredible because of what Charles Halt himself saw.

Certainly the best job of amalgamating all of the stories from the different witnesses on the night of December 27, 1980, into a coherent narrative was done by ufologist Jenny Randles, who spent over ten years researching the story for her book *UFO Crash Landing?* She even retrieved a copy of the audiotape that Charles Halt recorded that night while he was trekking through the forest in search of the strange lights from a UFO, a tape that documents some of the incredible eyewitness accounts of the happenings in the forest as Halt's unit searched for answers to the mystery of the glowing lights.

The night's events began, according to the accounts that Jenny Randles assembled from the witnesses, shortly before 10:30 P.M., when once again an Air Police patrol spotted lights over the trees outside the east gate. They radioed a report to the security desk manned by USAF Sergeant Adrian Bustinza, who in turn relayed the report to his superior, Lieutenant Bruce Englund, for permission to investigate the phenomenon. While Bustinza headed out to the east gate to see what the patrol had spotted, Lieutenant Englund thought it best to report directly to the base commander and deputy commander, who were at an officers' Christmas reception at RAF Woodbridge.

Pulling aside Colonel Conrad and Lieutenant Colonel Halt from the festivities, Lieutenant Englund whispered to them that a police unit along the base perimeter had spotted the lights over the forest again and that he'd already given permission for one of his sergeants to lead a security detail to where the lights had been spotted. Halt told his commanding officer that this time he'd clear the thing up once and for all, and told Englund that he'd go out there himself with as much equipment as he could muster. Clearly, Halt didn't expect to encounter a UFO, but he wanted to make sure that if base security was being compromised, he'd have enough personnel out there in the forest to get whatever evidence he could. He left the party to assemble his team, while Lieutenant Englund joined the security detail he'd posted along the east gate.

By the time Englund reached his men, other personnel had gathered beside the gate. News of the return of the strange lights had now spread across the base. Sergeant Bustinza had already taken a small group with him into the forest to find the location of the lights and radio it back to base security. He was about to have the same experience that confronted Sergeant Penniston the night before.

As Bustinza's small patrol approached the lights, which they could see glowing in colors through the trees, they were enveloped in a thick yellowish ground fog that swirled about their knees, curled into the cold night air, and clung to leaves like a heavy dew, chilling the entire forest into a deathly silence. Straight ahead of them they could see the object now, quietly flashing its multicolored lights and moving up and down as if it were hovering in the air. Sergeant Bustinza and the men in his group were struck with fear by the object. They approached slowly and with great caution until it started to float backward away from them.

Suddenly the object seemed to emit a pulse of electrical energy that made the forest animals burst into flight, chattering and screeching in fear as they bolted away from the object. Bustinza and his men were startled at first, and then they felt the effects of the electrical force field themselves. Bustinza later said that he could see the hair stand up straight on the heads of his men even though they were wearing protective gear.

At the same time that fear overwhelmed the group, they were given the order to withdraw from the forest as quickly as possible to reinforce Lieutenant Colonel Halt's team, which by now had assembled a number of self-powered lights, called light-alls, and was moving past the east gate to locate the object. Central Security didn't want independent groups traipsing through the forest, bumping into one another and possibly getting themselves hurt. Bustinza and his men pulled back very quickly, relieved at the order to vacate the area.

At 10:00 P.M. on another part of the base—even before Lieutenant Englund had arrived at the officer's Christmas party to alert the base commander and deputy commander to the lights over the forest—Airman Larry Warren was suiting up for his duty shift as a member of D Flight. He writes in *Left at East Gate* that his gear included a flak jacket, a chemical contamination suit, and a gas mask, all of which were inspected by his supervisor before the individual airmen on the watch were deposited by truck at their positions for the night. Some would remain at Bentwaters, others driven over to RAF Woodbridge. After inspection, Larry Warren was dropped off at one of the perimeter posts at the very end of the Bentwaters runway and stood guard, all alone, except for his radio, and silent, except for fifteen-minute status checks from the base Central Security Control.

Gradually the silence in the dark night on the flight line gave way to intermittent squawking through Airman Warren's radio speaker as he picked up fragments of transmissions between air police units around the base perimeter, who had seen some strange lights over the Rendlesham Forest. The transmissions about the floating lights got stranger as the voices of some of the incredulous air police began to crack with fear. They unnerved nineteen-year-old Airman Warren, who was on his first tour of duty outside the United States. He stood at his wind-whipped sentry post all alone on a cold moonless winter night as if he were at the end of the universe itself.

Soon the D Flight chief's "can the chatter" order blared through the speaker, and all went silent for a moment. Was that worse for Airman Warren or better? But his fear was interrupted, he says, by the wild sound of deer hooves clattering toward him in panic out of the darkness. Suddenly a small group of animals threw themselves toward the fence, two of them veering away and one bounding over it and running for its life across the flight line. Something was out there.

Larry Warren didn't have much time to wait before a pair of lights blinded him from down the runway, rushing toward him with an urgency that at this point matched his mood. It was a security police pickup truck with Sergeant Bustinza behind the wheel and Lieutenant Bruce Englund riding shotgun, two other security police officers sitting in the truck's bed. "You're relieved," Lieutenant Englund ordered Warren. "Radio this in to Central and tell them you're coming with us." Warren transmitted the lieutenant's order and received permission to leave the post. "Climb in back," Bustinza ordered, and told them they were heading over to the base motor pool to pick up light-alls for a security detail already under way.

Amid high tension and arguments at the motor pool, Larry Warren helped rig the light-all trailers to the trucks and gassed up the units. Meanwhile another pickup arrived at the motor pool and its crew attached an additional light-all, making sure that the truck's fuel tank and the generator's tank were both topped off. From the motor pool, Larry Warren's pickup, with Adrian Bustinza still behind the wheel, joined a small convoy of other security vehicles, all of them with their blue emergency lights on. The convoy left the perimeter gate and was quickly passed through a security roadblock that was holding back a few civilian vehicles. Now Larry Warren's suspicions were running wild. What could be the cause of this much security? Had Soviet troops invaded Poland again? Was there an attack on Woodbridge and Bentwaters, one of the primary staging areas for the A-10 tank buster squadrons that had already been moved to Germany just in case the Soviet armor pushed across the eastern border?

The convoy moved through Woodbridge, turned left at the east gate, and lumbered onto what Warren recognized as the narrow logging road into Rendlesham Forest. After they reached a clearing at the end of the dirt road, their trucks stopped and Larry Warren was ordered out of the back to stand ready for the next orders. Meanwhile, he could see that Lieutenant Englund had left the truck as soon as they pulled up and joined some other officers, including Lieutenant Colonel Halt inside the clearing. Warren and the other security police officers were told to maintain radio silence and listen for any orders. Then one of the officers waved them into the clearing and lined them up in a loose patrol formation behind a captain who was making his way toward something going on inside the clearing. But Larry Warren could see nothing from where he was standing.

Suddenly a ground flare broke the darkness of the night, and Warren could see powerful flashlights through the trees up ahead. Then he saw the figures of military personnel moving through the light, and that was when he came upon the first area cordoned off by orange tape. The line kept on moving deeper into the forest—a hundred feet, a thousand feet, a quarter of a mile—as the radio transmissions back and forth became more ominous. Something had happened out there, that was the reason for all this tape and the orders to avoid the taped areas. Suddenly, as Sergeant Bustinza appeared to get very nervous, Larry Warren's group entered an area of dense yellow-green ground fog illuminated by something in the clearing down the path. Ahead of them they could see a pair of officers with Geiger counters sweeping the area of the fog. What were they heading into?

Just as they came to the open clearing, Larry Warren was amazed at the sight of a multicolored object, seemingly on the ground but vaguely moving up and down, right in front of them. Movie camera operators stood to either side filming whatever this object was. Through the open speakers, Warren could hear lots of radio transmissions telling him that, clearly, the base knew what was going on and that whatever he was doing in the clearing with the other security personnel and what looked like senior brass up ahead, this was no drill. It was some sort of security intrusion, and a select group of people from his flight along with some of the senior officers had been mobilized to deal with it.

His body growing heavy and his breathing labored as he stood in the clearing, Warren noticed a bright red light bearing westward as it flew over the forest from the direction of the North Sea. A radio speaker blared, "Here it comes," and all eyes shot up to see the light as it approached them. Were they under attack? But nobody moved. Instead they watched the light as it followed a trajectory over the tops of the trees and into the clearing. There it came to a hovering stop maybe twenty or so feet over the fog that had spread out along the ground and which had partially enveloped the strange object in the clearing. The light simply hung in the air.

While the assembled air force personnel stared at the red light, not knowing what to make of it, it exploded, Warren said, into a thousand bits of light that rained down on the fog. When their night vision returned, the military security teams could see that the fog was largely dissipated and they were staring at a large pyramid-shaped object with a red light on top standing in the middle of the clearing. It was clearly a machine of some sort, Warren thought, but he had never seen its like be-

fore. If he looked at it directly, it seemed that its shape
was changing. It was standing on some sort of landing
gear or legs, Warren thought, but these were obscured
by the blue lights along the bottom rim. From his position, maybe twenty feet away from the thing, he could
see what he would later describe in his narrative as "delta
like appendages" jutting out from the main body of the
object that gave it an "almost threatening appearance."

The same force field that had affected Penniston on
the first night and Bustinza earlier in the evening was
now affecting Warren. He said that he wanted to throw
up inside his helmet and that the hair all over his body
was standing up as if charged with electricity. Whatever
it was, it was disorienting to all of the men. Then a senior officer gave the order to secure the entire area around
the machine with a tight cordon. This, Warren explained,
was a normal procedure to prevent any security breach
of an area containing a nuclear device. It signified that
the air force team on this site meant business.

Then another officer ordered him forward to accompany one of the nuclear biological chemical disaster people who was carrying a Geiger counter. As they reached
the object, maybe ten feet away, Warren said he couldn't
even focus his eyes on the machine because they were
watering so much. The entire scene was unreal. He
looked at the way his shadow played against the object's glow. This was bizarre because there was no light
behind him to throw a shadow forward. And then, in a
manner almost subtly terrifying, as if he were watching
it in a Stephen King movie, his shadow seemed to move
across the surface of the object before he did.

Warren was becoming weak in the knees from fear

of the unknown object in front of him. Finally he was ordered to return to his original position along a twenty-foot perimeter, and his fear eased a bit. From the corner of his eye, he could see both military personnel and police officers from the local village of Woodbridge converge at the edge of the clearing. Then the police set up a motion picture camera, which the air force security teams pulled away from them. Fights were breaking out all over the perimeter of the clearing and the situation was quickly descending into pandemonium while a few officers acted as if they were following a plan that didn't concern anyone else in the clearing. Then a staff car was escorted to the edge of the clearing, and Warren could see some of the officers snap to attention.

The cordon of security personnel parted to allow the staff officers through the perimeter, and Larry Warren believed he saw the 81st Tactical Fighter Wing commander Colonel Gordon Williams and other officers on his staff emerge. He thought he saw Lieutenant Colonel Halt as well, though the officers were not in uniform. In fact, it looked to Warren as if the officers, the wing commander and the deputy base commander were in fancy clothes, as if they'd just come from a party. The officers huddled for a moment and then stood in front of the glowing object.

A ball of light seemed to emerge from behind the object, Larry Warren observed, floating just above the ground and moving toward the group of senior officers standing about ten feet in front of the large object. Warren thought he could see figures inside, and Sergeant Bustinza seemed to be whispering something about seeing "kids" and asked Warren if he could see them. Warren later said that these weren't kids, at least not kids that he'd ever seen before. The light separated into three distinct orbs, Warren said, each containing one creature inside. They just hung in the air in front of the officers, who, though nervous, seemed to know that they had to be there.

The creatures inside the orbs were small, about four feet tall, and dressed in what looked like silvery one-piece flight suits. They had overly large black eyes that were the dominant feature on their faces. And they just waited until Wing Commander Williams stepped up and looked down at them. To Airman Warren, the creatures seemed to be communicating with Gordon Williams even though Williams didn't speak and Warren couldn't hear any sound coming from the creatures in the orbs. Finally, after Williams conferred with officers huddled behind him two or three times, the creatures got even closer to the colonel as the cordon of troops around the perimeter of the clearing began to break up. Larry Warren was directed away from the scene. As he left to get back on the truck, he could see Colonel Williams still engaged with the creatures in the orbs.

Once outside the clearing, Larry Warren could see lots of lights flying overhead, shooting blue beams down through the trees as if they were looking for something. The entire sky was filled with darting lights, and details of security personnel crashed through the forest looking for other places where the lights might have landed. Warren could hear noises all around him as he climbed into the bed of his pickup and was driven back to the base. Meanwhile, other security parties remained in the forest until all the lights had departed, shortly before sunup.

Colonel Halt's Audiotape

Lieutenant Colonel Halt tells a very different story from the one reported by Larry Warren. Maybe the two of them had real but very different encounters; for a time they were in different places of the forest. Larry Warren doesn't say that he sees Colonel Halt during the entire period in the clearing in the same way that he says he saw Wing Commander Colonel Williams seem to communicate with the aliens. Lieutenant Colonel Halt's account is also buttressed by a tape recording he made as he mustered his team out to the forest to investigate the lights. Halt remembered that as he assembled his gear for the late-night trek, he grabbed his pocket tape recorder so he could dictate notes that would be used later for his official report.

While Larry Warren was heading out to the clearing in Adrian Bustinza's truck, Colonel Halt's team had already made it into the forest. But their own light-alls had begun to fail. That was the reason for the order to Lieutenant Englund to hook up another light-all to his truck and bring it out to the clearing with the rest of the security convoy.

Halt took his team to the area where Penniston had seen the object settle to the ground on legs or struts and then rise through the trees. While Englund's group headed for the clearing where they had been told lights had already settled on the ground, Halt inspected the indentations on the ground for residual heat traces and radiation. His operators discovered high concentrations of radiation within the triangular impression marks and a heat residue not only on the ground but through an opening in the trees. Even Halt, looking up through the opening and noticing the pattern of broken and pushed-back tree limbs, realized that something was very unnatural about it. It looked to him as if an object might have passed through, but the narrow shaft of damage couldn't have been made by any conventional aircraft.

A sudden explosion of animal howls and screeches caught Halt's attention—probably the same noises that Larry Warren reported when the object in the clearing generated an electrical energy force field burst. Then the radio operator picked up a transmission from base about incoming lights, and they looked up to see lights heading toward the clearing, a whole array of lights floating over an area of the forest approximately a quarter mile in front of them. Halt remarked that he was amazed at the strangeness of the situation because one of the lights broke away from the others and seemed to be coming out of the sky directly at them. It was red, he said, and at the center seemed to have a dark spot that resembled an eye. There is a similarity between Larry Warren's characterization of the sphere he saw as having dark centers containing life-forms with huge black eyes and Halt's description of the glowing red light with the dark center that looked like an eye.

Jenny Randles has pointed out that the winking light prompted skeptics to argue that Halt and the others were merely following the light from Orford Ness lighthouse, an argument that has persisted to this day. But Randles also correctly points out that these were military personnel who had often seen the Orford Ness lighthouse and wouldn't confuse it with a glowing red light. Besides, why would the animals panic as if in a frenzy over a lighthouse light that was a part of their daily environment? No, the red light that was descending over Halt's unit in the forest, and the other lights that were hovering over the clearing where Larry Warren observed them, were very different from the Orford Ness lighthouse.

Colonel Halt ordered his team to follow the direction of the cluster of lights heading toward the clearing where Bruce Englund's convoy had assembled. Suddenly the noise of the forest died away completely and everything went silent. It was as if a pall had descended over everything. Then, as Halt reached the edge of the clearing, one of his men told him that there was a large object on the ground, and he saw the red light explode into shards, probably the same event that Larry Warren reported.

Halt's men followed other darting lights through the forest, pushing on past the clearing and the glowing object, as they headed toward the coast. Halt also reported laserlike beams of light shooting down from the sky as if looking for something or probing the area. Another one of his men described the beams as blue, which is exactly what Larry Warren remembered seeing as he and his team were pulled back from the clearing by their superiors and sent back to the base.

What could these lights be? Halt remembers thinking to himself. Were they probes that weren't intended to harm anyone in the forest that night, or were they weapons? He remembers that they continued for a while as his team headed for the coast in the direction of the lights. Halt says that at about four in the morning, he couldn't resolve what the lights were, there was nothing he could do to stop them, and the men on his team were exhausted. He finally pulled them out of the forest and went back to Bentwaters, where he would compile his dictated notes into a memo for the base commander.

Halt's memo, the audiotape he recorded, and the testimonies of most of the men who were in Rendlesham Forest those nights at the end of December 1980 would be immediately buried under layers of secrecy even as the stories of some of the local residents and radar operators began to spread in early 1981. As tales circulated and rumors began to inflate what might have been true into wild science fiction, a number of investigators, including UFO researcher Jenny Randles, British science writer Ian Ridpath, and even the UK Ministry of Defense specialist on UFOs, Nick Pope, all began their own inquiries. Nick Pope, who later wrote *Open Skies, Closed Minds,* in which he argues that the evidence for UFO encounters with the world's military and with governments is overwhelming despite the official denials, and Jenny Randles remain convinced that there was something out of the ordinary in Rendlesham Forest, whether it was extraterrestrial or part of a top secret emergency military preparedness exercise. Ian Ridpath, however, became convinced that the lights were simply the beacon from the Orford Ness lighthouse, which looked into Rendlesham Forest from a spit of land on the coast. It was the disorientation of the men and a dense but very natural ground fog that resulted in the panic.

The Orford Ness Lighthouse

Ian Ridpath argued from the start that Colonel Halt's account of his eastward trek through the woods to the coast, following a winking light, sounded suspiciously as if Halt were actually following the rotating beacon from the Orford Ness lighthouse, which lay directly ahead of him on the course he was taking. UFO researchers have argued that the light Halt was following was red while the Orford Ness light is white. Ridpath writes that Halt's own men disagreed with him and that the light was actually a yellowish white, which it could have seemed had the light been refracted by the ground fog billowing up around them. The daytime temperatures were in the forties but dropped quickly into the low thirties in the evening, which could have created a fog layer along the damp forest floor. The beam reflecting off the fog bank could have given it a yellowish hue as the moisture in the fog broke the white light into its constituent colors. Ridpath also said that the light was shining near enough to the farmer's house where Larry Warren noticed lights that the house might have obscured the lighthouse itself but not the beacon.

As for the other lights darting back and forth in the sky, Jenny Randles suggests that Halt and his men were only looking at stars and, in trying to pinpoint them against the black sky, were experiencing an illusion called autokinesis, in which the eye, trying to capture an image that's on the retina, darts back and forth. This quick eye movement tricks the brain into thinking that the object itself is moving when in fact it's really the eye that's moving. (You can try to replicate this illusion yourself by staring intently at a faint star in the night sky. If you fixate on it for a few minutes, you'll get the impression that the star is moving. In reality it's your eye that's moving, trying to keep the star in focus.)

However, Jenny Randles also points out that Ridpath's argument about the lighthouse fails, given the descriptions of the object on the ground that seemed to have a dark center. And she says that Halt's description on his audiocassette of a liquid or "molten" quality to the light seems to indicate that he was looking at the light through an energy field. And although Halt maintains a professional military demeanor in his recording of the events in the forest that night, his voice on the tape reflects an intense emotion as he sees a light he can neither identify nor explain. She says that Halt, an experienced military observer, and other members of the team who'd served at Bentwaters for considerable periods of time were more than used to the lighthouse and had seen enough of the beacon to be able to distinguish it from a completely strange light. Besides, she argues, both Halt's team and Larry Warren's group saw the red light come to them and then break into pieces. And nothing that Ridpath has argued can speak for the descriptions given by Penniston, Bustinza, and Larry Warren of the object that hovered above the forest and then shot off into the sky. The impressions on the ground, she suggests, far from being rabbit holes or animal tracks, showed residual radiation, as did the shaftway through the trees made by the object Penniston saw when it took off. Perhaps at some point they saw the lighthouse beacon, she concedes, but they certainly didn't mistake it for whatever object might have actually been on the ground.

A Military Exercise?

After all the cover-up and testimony, after all the therapy to recover hidden memories, after all the arguments and counterarguments, we still can only ask, what had the witnesses seen? Why were there film crews in the middle of the forest, and where is the film today? Larry Warren believed he saw aliens inside the spheres. Who were they and where were they from? And was this a prearranged meeting between military personnel and extraterrestrials or had the UFOs simply appeared without warning? For twenty years the veracity of the Bentwaters incident has been debated in both the United Kingdom and the United States, but no definitive answers have emerged despite the incredible tape from Lieutenant Colonel Halt that the U.S. Air Force ultimately released. And the air force's release of that tape actually poses even more questions than it was supposed to answer.

Why would the U.S. military, after over fifty years of denial regarding UFOs, ultimately release an audio that, if anything, supported the argument that UFOs exist? Why would they release this audio when, just eleven years earlier, the air force had asked Professor Edward Condon who was head of the Colorado Report panel to debunk UFOs so that the air force could kill its own Project Blue Book? Logic seems to fail—unless there is a deeper, more sinister reason behind what went on at Bentwaters.

It's a reason that Jenny Randles herself suggests, and which is further supported from material hidden in the personal memoir of Lieutenant General Arthur Trudeau, the former head of U.S. Army Intelligence (G-2), who briefly describes the kinds of experimentation the army conducted on enlisted personnel and officer staff with nonlethal weapons. The idea of a military exercise in which only a few of the participants had any knowledge of what was going on is suggested by the CIA's experiments with nonlethal psychological weapons as well.

Just possibly, at a period of growing tension in Europe, when Soviet troops were on the move in Europe as well as active in Afghanistan and deploying microwave-directed energy weapons against the Mujahadeen in order to disable them, NATO decided not only to test their own versions of nonlethal energy field weapons but to see how military personnel might react in real time to a test of what an enemy might do. Would Allied, particularly American, forces advance toward an unknown but presumed hostile objective even when debilitated by a weapon that produced strange sensations? Could a series of distorted visual signals—projections or holographs—confuse highly trained U.S. security personnel? At what point would Americans break and run before an unknown enemy, and could strange visions of bizarre or terrifying events be implanted into the memories of selected military personnel so as to spread destabilizing rumors through an entire military command? Could this have been the objective of a test at Bentwaters?

This was the final decade of the cold war. Americans were being held hostage in Tehran. The Soviets had snubbed warnings of dire consequences made by President Jimmy Carter. The Solidarity movement in Poland was threatening the very sovereignty of Iron Curtain military powers that the Soviets had assembled in the years after World War II. This would have been an ideal time frame to test the reactions of American support, security, and logistics troops at an air base outside the United States, away from the prying eyes of American reporters.

Why use UFOs? Many psychological warfare experts suggest that UFOs make the ideal scare weapon because Americans have become conditioned to the possibility of flying saucers. UFOs are bona fide unknowns whose intentions are in question. By creating the scenario of a UFO landing in a secure area, American commanders would have an excellent war game test of whether troops assigned to base security would perform as they had been trained under a state of panic. In the case of Bentwaters, the debriefings that Larry Warren described in *Left at East Gate* were designed to see how he had reacted while at the same time scaring him into silence.

The United States has tested varieties of weapons on its personnel since the end of World War II. They exposed GIs to atomic radiation, tried to figure out how Soviet and Chinese interrogators broke the spirits of captured U.S. pilots during the Korean War, and engaged in everything from clumsy to sophisticated testing of psychotropic chemicals on Americans—even members of the Army General Staff, according to Arthur Trudeau—in the 1950s. In defending in his memoirs the army's use of psychotropic drug testing on its personnel, Trudeau was adamant that if the army could learn to disrupt the command system through psychological intervention it would save lives by rendering enemy troops defenseless.

Thus, assuming that the United States actually had the technology to create the effects, Bentwaters could have been a psychological warfare exercise, complete with the use of energy field weapons or directed microwave weapons that, according to the writers of the French COMETA report (see Chapter 10), were being tested at U.S. military laboratories. We had the capability to test a microwave or energy field weapon under controlled circumstances while the Soviets were already prepared to deploy microwave weapons in Afghanistan. It would be a perfect test.

The military knew that once somebody shouted "flying saucers," nobody would believe the next words out of his mouth. Since the late 1940s the American government and the media had done such an excellent job conditioning most people to look at flying saucers as a joke and humiliating anyone who took them seriously, people who'd been subjected to the test would be very reluctant to talk about it. Even the late Colonel Philip Corso (author of *The Day After Roswell*) said ufologists would do a better job of debunking themselves than any government could manage. Maybe that's why the air force was so willing to release the Halt memo from 1981. Who would believe it? And, if it was a setup, maybe the memo would do more to cover up the operation than a denial would.

That still leaves us with the question, What happened at Bentwaters and why? We know that the Bentwaters and Woodbridge air defense complex had had an encounter with unidentified flying objects twenty-five years earlier. As described in the French COMETA report, in 1956 an object traveling southeast at an estimated air speed of 4,000 mph was picked up on defense radars and stayed on the screen for about thirty seconds. A second sighting, this time a formation of unidentified objects, was picked up traveling northeast. Then there were a third and a fourth sighting, as well as visual sightings from the ground, and RAF Venom aircraft scrambled to intercept and chase. When the objects disappeared, the reports were typed up, filed, and then allowed to drift into history. Is that why Bentwaters might have been chosen as a test site in 1980?

Unfortunately, the answer is that we still don't know. Part of the mystery is the continuing official denial that anything took place at all. Ian Ridpath is a convenient debunker, but the lighthouse and an autokinetic response to stars explain only a fraction of what the witnesses, including Colonel Halt, say went on there that night. One could argue that the area had already drawn a UFO incursion in the 1950s and was therefore a site to be re-visited by extraterrestrial aircraft. But one could also say that the kinds of technology that were already in development by 1980 conceivably lend credence to the kind of psychological warfare test that you'd only read about in a Tom Clancy political thriller. One has to conclude, therefore—if we discount the lighthouse explanation because it accounts for only one light—that the Bentwaters case was either a bona fide UFO sighting or an induced mass hallucination that, whether or not it involved the complicity of some senior staff officers, certainly involved enough enlisted personnel and junior officers that one only hopes the air force got the results it was looking for. What is more incredible, a UFO or a bizarre high-tech psychological weapons test? The answers may still lie somewhere in the top secret file of what happened that night. And until it's declassified and released, we may never know.

CHAPTER 6

Alien Implants

"I certainly believe in aliens in space. They may not look like us, but I have very strong feelings that they have advanced beyond our mental capabilities. . . . I think some highly secret government UFO investigations are going on that we don't know about—and probably never will unless the Air Force discloses them."

Senator Barry Goldwater

WITNESSES DESCRIBE THEIR FIRSTHAND UFO SIGHTINGS as "awe-inspiring," "astonishing"; the most fantastic displays they have seen in their entire lives. A review of many of the audio tracks from the private Phoenix Lights videos captures the wonder and amazement as the procession of lights traveled across the sky. When the strange lights seem to interact with the witnesses, as they did with Ed Walters in Gulf Breeze and Larry Warren and other military personnel at RAF Bentwaters, manifesting the entities' collective awareness of a witness's presence by throwing off a new sequence of lights, directing a strange beam at the ground as if it were a police helicopter searchlight, or darting out of the heavens in an instant to hover only a few feet directly over a human being, it can be frightening.

But what witnesses and those who call themselves "experiencers" have reported as truly terrifying is an actual transportation from everyday reality into the world of the creatures inside the UFO. One minute, some have said, you see something out of the ordinary in the sky, and the next thing you know you're trapped on an examination table with strange beings hovering over you, or else devastated by the memory of a terrifying vision that you feel in the pit of your stomach might actually have been real. Therapists and researchers call this nightmare journey to the inside of a craft an alien abduction.

Personal encounters with UFOs and the people who navigate them, encounters that come in the form of being transported into the belly of the aliens' lair, have their own categories and characteristics. There are people who claim that these encounters are more like spiritual bonding rituals in which the aliens reveal themselves to be the allies of humanity. Others see the experiences as a traumatic wrenching out of one existence into another. And still others describe sexual probes in the guise of medical experiments, the harvesting of ova and sperm, and the hybridizing of a new species. And there are even those who make another claim. These experiencers describe themselves as "implantees": individuals who are inserted with a subcutaneous device which either tracks the subject or monitors some other physiological or psychological functions.

In the world of unsolved UFO mysteries, abduction and implant stories remain the most puzzling and challenging. That's why the UFO community took notice when Dr. Roger Leir, a podiatric surgeon from Ventura County, California, reported that he had removed a strange implant from a person who had claimed abduction experiences. Some doubted him and called his reports fanciful. But others, especially organizations that funded UFO research, found plenty to discuss in what Dr. Leir had discovered. Even Roger Leir would suggest that in order to understand the nature of alien implants, one has to understand the general nature of alien abductions, what the abductees report as their experiences, and how they were able to recover their memories.

Abductions

If we discount the wild stories of George Adamsky and his flights to the planet Venus, which he vividly described in magazine articles in the 1950s, one of the first abduction therapy cases can be traced back to a brisk New England evening in the early autumn of 1961. Barney and Betty Hill were driving home along a country road when they noticed a distant light near the horizon begin to change shape. As they watched incredulously, the light became a flat saucerlike object displaying a line of windows along the exterior rim. It seemed to take notice of them and flew right at them out of the sky. As the saucer-shaped craft loomed overhead, Barney Hill stopped the car, looked through his binoculars, and caught his breath. He believed he could see people looking at him as if they were peering out of apartment windows onto the street below. Now he was frightened.

So he got back into the car, revved the engine, and floored it out of there as fast as he could.

The last thing Barney Hill remembered was a strange, rhythmic beeping in his ears, and the next thing he knew he and his wife Betty were driving up the narrow road to their house. But he couldn't account for how he got there. Maybe he fell asleep at the wheel, he thought, it could happen. But then he realized he'd been on the road for hours, hours longer than it should have taken him to get home, and that there was a space of time he couldn't have accounted for even if he'd pulled off to the side of the road for a quick catnap.

Betty Hill was similarly at a loss. She didn't remember the journey. Had they both fallen asleep and lost all track of the passage of time? It felt as if something had happened to them, but neither Betty nor Barney could figure out exactly what that was, only that they'd somehow missed about two or so hours out of their lives.

Over the course of the next couple of weeks, Betty began to experience strange nightmares, dreams of terror unlike any she'd ever had before. And for some odd reason Barney's ulcers were acting up again. He thought those ulcers were well under control, and they only caused him a problem when he was having undue stress. What was behind all this? The doctors couldn't find anything physically wrong with him that would give him such discomfort; maybe he had an underlying problem that only a psychiatrist could address. So Betty and Barney Hill made an appointment and discovered something that made them unwitting international celebrities and the reluctant representatives of a whole new group.

Dr. Benjamin Simon, a psychiatrist with no predisposition toward the supernatural, began what should have been a normal regression process to get to the root of what might be disturbing Barney. What underlying thoughts were eating away at him, creating stress and churning the acid that was chewing away at his stomach and intestinal walls? As they stepped backward in time over the weeks to when Barney's discomfort and Betty's dreams began, they wound up on the September night when the Hills were driving home. That was when the doctor discovered they couldn't account for a few hours of the journey. Could this be the culprit?

What a shock it was when, as Dr. Simon asked Barney where he was, his patient began to describe a strange group of gray creatures who laid him out on a table and extracted sperm from him. It was a violent sexual assault, he said, strapped to a table in a semitrance state but aware of the terror of strange hands on his genitals measuring out seminal fluid while a harsh light burned into his eyes. And Betty's experience was no less terrifying. She described a long needle being inserted into her abdomen while voices inside her head told her not to fight. As she described the strange medical procedure and Dr. Simon marveled at the detail and precision of her recall, what neither she nor her psychiatrist realized was that she was describing something that would become almost common in the next decade: amniocentesis.

The Hills had described an abduction complete with missing time, medical experiments, and the posttraumatic stress many abductees experience. They learned that this was not their first abduction experience, and that they, like others who would come after them, were caught in some grim cross-breeding experiment that the gray aliens were conducting on this planet for their own purposes.

Over the course of the next thirty years America would be fascinated by a variety of abduction stories told by individuals who would seem to be the most normal of normal: nighttime outdoorsmen taking a canoe trip who were beamed up into a spacecraft; two fishermen from Pascagoula, Mississippi, who suddenly found themselves under the power of alien creatures; a good old boy named Travis Walton who, in sight of his friends (who drove away as if they were fleeing the devil) was caught and paralyzed in a beam of light and held in the slimy human cargo bay of an alien craft until the inhabitants were through with him; and a woman transported to a spacecraft from right in the middle of New York City. Abductees told stories of bizarre encounters with hybrid children who needed nurturing from their human parents, insightful messages from alien creatures who instructed them to impart their knowledge to their fellow human beings, and other stories about galactic wars between extraterrestrial species that would soon be played out on planet Earth.

In the 1980s, therapist and UFO researcher Budd Hopkins gave us a language for abductions in his book *Missing Time,* and author Whitley Streiber described his experiences as an abductee in *Communion.* Although ostensibly a work of fiction, the latter terrified readers because it put a tangible face on the nameless aliens, who, Streiber revealed, had shadowed him throughout his life ever since he was a child. And in the 1990s both David Jacobs from Temple University and Dr. Jonathan Mack from Harvard revealed a dark side to alien abductions through their research with individuals. They suggested that alien abductions were far more insidious and routine than most people believed and revealed a level of alien interaction with humans that went far beyond a casual roadstop on a hot Indiana summer night.

UFO Magazine writer Mike Miley, in his article on the nature of alien abduction, describes not only the prototypical abduction scenario but cites witness testimony that there are more alien species out there than just the "grays" that were made famous in science-fiction movies. Miley cites the work of David Jacobs and Thomas Bullard in his description of a basic story structure that underlies most abduction reports.

The experiencer describes these basic elements: (1) Capture, (2) an examination or probe, (3) some form of enlightenment, which may or may not be accompanied by a description or vision of the "other world" but which is usually in the form of an imparting of knowledge and sometimes involves the implanting of a strange device, (4) a return to this world, and (5) some posttraumatic period of recovery in which the experiencer may or may not have a memory loss that requires some form of therapy.

In many abduction scenarios, the experiencer has returned with the device still intact, a hard souvenir of his or her otherworldly experience, the "Golden Bough" of Aeneas.

Skeptics abound, of course, and explain the eerie capture scenarios in which the witness feels paralyzed, drowsy, and unable to resist as a form of sleep paralysis. The dream vision is akin not only to the visitations of spirits in classical literature, but to the dream vision in medieval literature as well. It's no more than a dream, skeptics say, vivid but completely explainable in psychological terms. People who are abducted usually have other events going on in their lives that render them vulnerable, or perhaps they are otherwise lost souls seeking a greater meaning. "Nobody abducts the Beaver," some have said, indicating that people with relatively well-integrated personalities may sometimes face hardship and trauma, but all of it remains on planet Earth.

If all of this is so subjective and can be recovered only by the most subjective of therapies, hypnotic regression, where can we find any hard evidence that abductions have taken place at all? Many researchers point to the basic commonalities of the abduction experience, the abduction paradigm itself, as a piece of evidence: that people who don't know each other can describe exactly the same scenarios. Others point to the similarities in people's descriptions of the creatures who abducted them. And still others point to the one piece of physical evidence that sometimes remains for many years inside abductees' bodies: the metal implant that was inserted during the abduction itself.

Implant Stories

Abduction therapists point to the bruises and bumps some abductees discover on their bodies after periods of missing time, or in the morning upon awakening, as real physical evidence that something has happened to them. When abductees find these marks, they realize their feelings of extreme psychological discomfort or actual dread may be

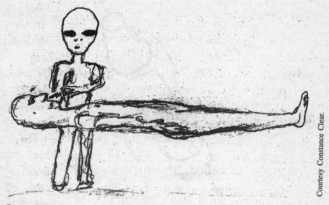

Some abductees, especially those who have been implanted with strange devices, report being suspended in air and operated on. This is an artist's rendition of an abductee's experience.

Courtesy Constance Clear.

traced to an occurrence that has become lost to their conscious memories. Sometimes the bruises are really scars that look like little scoops or scallops in the skin. Budd Hopkins has referred to them as "scoop marks" and says they result from skin being removed from the abductee. Other people report finding blood on their pillows as if they'd injured the inner parts of their ears or had a nosebleed during the night. Therapists have said that these injuries, as well as bruises, contusions, and types of skin discolorations, mean that the person reporting the abduction experience was also the victim of some type of medical experiment at the hands of the aliens.

Some abductees have complained to doctors that after vaguely remembered nightmares from which they've awakened feeling violated, they have persistent memories of metal probes being inserted into their noses or

Courtesy Constance Clear.

Detail of implant device.

skulls. Others talk about strange sensations in their legs
or hands and even state that when they run their hands
over the spots they feel lumps. More than one doctor
has said that these are bruises from bumping into a bed-
post or a night table and they'll go away. And for the
overwhelming majority of people they do go away. But,
like a bad penny that keeps turning up, the sensations
of lumpiness or a bruise that becomes hard remain with
the victims and they can't explain why.

For some who awaken from the dream with a clear
memory of an object being inserted under the skin, there
is no expectation that the feeling will go away. One abductee said that he felt the object was a part of him,
and even though he believed it was a kind of violation

to have a foreign body lodged under his skin, he'd feel kind of lonely without it. Maybe that's exactly the sensation whoever implanted the object wanted him to feel. But the debate over the existence of alien implants persisted among the abductee community and therapists for years before some therapists decided to confront whatever the truth was and see if what abductees called implants were really there. For one California surgeon with a passing interest in UFOs, the question came to a head at a UFO convention. That's where he was approached by an abduction therapist who challenged him to review the file of an individual who claimed that she'd been implanted and had X rays taken to prove it.

Implant Doctor

The California surgeon whose life took a dramatic change because of a set of mysterious X rays was Dr. Roger Leir, a flying enthusiast and private pilot who had built a successful podiatric practice in Thousand Oaks. He remembers the day the newspapers carried the headline of a UFO crash in Roswell, and the day they retracted it. His father, who had brought the evening paper home from work, pointed to the weather balloon story on the first page—the story the army put out to explain what had crashed in Roswell—and complained that the government was always covering up something. That was Roger Leir's introduction to flying saucers.

Years later, after Roger Leir had become a practicing surgeon, that interest in flying saucers stayed with him. He joined MUFON and was an active participant in meetings and lectures about the presence of UFOs and what their existence might imply. He wasn't directly involved with the abductee community. But that all changed at a UFO conference in California where he met another UFO researcher named Derrel Sims. Sims described his own direct work with abductees, not only in helping them recover memories lost during the abduction process, but finding methods to help them actively resist their abductors.

In his conversation with Leir, Sims described the complaints of some of his clients, who said that their alien captors had implanted objects in their bodies. In one woman's case, Sims said, the object had been embedded for a while, but the woman couldn't get anyone to take it out.

"Impossible," Dr. Leir responded. Any foreign object large enough to be an irritant would be forced out if it was just under the skin. Or it would cause inflammations or infections, and there'd be a host of adjacent symptoms as the body tried to reject a foreign presence. But Sims persisted to the point where Leir finally said he'd have to see the X rays before saying anything else. At that point Sims pulled out the woman's medical file and opened it in front of Leir. And there were the X rays.

Leir held the film up to the light. There were two objects embedded in the woman's toe, one looking like a small melon seed and the other a rough "T" shape. "No way," he said to Sims. You couldn't have objects like this inside something as small as a toe without scarring, an entry wound, an inflammation in the spot where the body is trying to reject it. These objects would have caused her a great discomfort, Leir explained. Even if she'd stepped on a nail or gotten a piece of metal lodged in her toe, there would have been such a reaction that she'd have gone to a doctor to get it extracted. The only explanation—though the X rays didn't support it—was that some piece of a surgical implement had been left behind inside after an operation on her toe. But, Sims said, the woman claimed she'd never had surgery there.

"So did she say how it got in there?" Dr. Leir asked.

Sims stared at him stone-faced and said, "She has no memory of it being implanted." Sims explained that although she had recalled an abduction encounter, it was only when she had her foot X-rayed in connection with a different medical problem that the radiologist discovered the objects in her toe.

There was only one way to determine the nature of these objects inside the patient, Leir explained, and that was to extract them surgically and see what they were made of. If it was a piece of scrap metal from an accident she'd forgotten about, they'd know it when they pulled it out and analyzed it. "Tell you what," Leir offered. "If she can get her way paid to California, I'll set up the surgery for free and we'll get it analyzed."

And they struck a deal. Derrel Sims would get the patient—or *patients,* because he had another candidate, a male, who had experienced a UFO encounter when he was a child and had only recently discovered an implant in his finger—to California. Dr. Leir would set up the surgical procedure under all kinds of medical and scientific controls with witnesses present. They would record the entire operation on videotape and present the results to the scientific community. At the end of it, each man expected, they'd have a piece of hard evidence. Either it would be an anomalous object or they would find a completely mundane piece of scrap that, at the very least, would no longer be inside the patient's toe.

Roger Leir had never expected that he'd find himself in the alien abduction business, not to mention the extraction of extraterrestrial implants business. So he had to prepare. He retained the services of a general surgeon to perform any procedures on the patient above the foot, an anesthesiologist to administer a local to the area where Leir and his surgical partner would probe, a surgical nurse, a number of witnesses, Derrel Sims—who was also a certified hypnoanesthesiologist—an attorney, psychologist Barbara Dobrin, and both still and video photographers. Leir wanted to keep a minute-by-minute record of the surgery, because, as he's said in a number of interviews, including a conversation with *UFO Magazine,* "Let's face it, if you're a doctor saying you're removing implants from people who've been abducted by extraterrestrials, you want anyone to be able to see the complete surgical procedure from start to finish." He also needed to document the chain of evidence of whatever it was he extracted so there would be no doubt in anyone's mind that what he pulled out of the patient was the exact same object that was sent off to a laboratory for testing.

The Surgery

Before the first local anesthetic was administered, before the first scalpel was raised, Roger Leir took an-

other set of X rays of the objects he was going to extract, just to double check their location. Then he and
Derrel Sims asked the patients to provide another complete description of their abduction experiences, but this
time to relate their stories to psychologist Barbara Dobrin. They spoke to her separately and didn't share stories with one another. The UFO researchers wanted to
make sure that the two abduction stories, as different
as they were, didn't cross-pollinate one another with
new information.

Dr. Leir also examined the female patient's foot thoroughly to look for any entry wounds or scars. He expected to find a mark at or near the surface; he wanted
to be able to determine whether the object had moved
inside the patient and how far it lay from the original
point of entry. Yet—and he was in for a shock when he
realized this—there was no entry wound. Anything that
penetrates the skin deep enough to lodge below the surface, even a splinter, leaves a trace wound somewhere
that becomes scarred over. Yet here was a sizable object—no, two objects—lodged in a patient's toe and neither object had a corresponding entry wound that he
could see. This defied logic and was the beginning of
the abnormal sequence of events that Dr. Leir would experience during the next two hours of surgery.

After his visual examination and a review of the new
X rays, Dr. Leir extracted small quantities of blood from
each patient. He prepared a blood serum medium to preserve the objects so they could remain in the same types
of bodily fluids during transport to a testing facility.
With the blood serum tubes ready, the cameras started
rolling and the first patient, the woman with objects in

her toe, received a heavy dose of local anesthetic to deaden the nerves in her toe completely.

Then Derrel Sims went to work. He had worked with this woman previously in order to help her recover her lost abduction memories and induced what he described as an anesthetic trance. Not only was she relaxed about the operation on her foot, she was completely anesthetized and confident that she would feel no pain during the procedure.

As expected, the patient reported no pain during the initial incision. She remained completely relaxed as the surgical team prepared the point of entry for a deep probe to locate and remove the objects. Guided by the brand-new set of X rays, Dr. Leir began to probe the incision for the first of the pieces.

The "melon seed," as they called it, should have been relatively near the surface of the skin. But as Dr. Leir probed closer to where he believed the object was lying, he began to feel that the woman's foot was tensing up. That was strange. She was chemically anesthetized to the point where he could have performed major surgery on her foot. Also, Derrel Sims had assured him that she was in a very deep hypnotic state in which she should have had no feeling whatsoever in the area of the surgery. So what could she be reacting to on the table? Maybe it was the pressure. He continued to probe gently until the tip of his instrument reached the area where the first object was. The patient groaned and tensed, and her eyelids fluttered in discomfort. Derrel Sims calmed her down with suggestions to relax, and she seemed to settle back. Then Roger Leir probed further until he finally hit the object.

The woman screamed in pain and terror as the object moved under the pressure of the surgical instrument, and she jerked her foot back, sending the probe flying across the operating room. Her body convulsed in spasm as if she'd received a Frankenstein bolt of electric shock. The operation stopped dead while Derrel Sims tried to hold the woman's body on the table.

"We'd given her enough anesthetic to take down a horse," Leir later said about the incident. "And Derrel Sims had her completely relaxed. There was no medical reason I can think of for her to have felt any sensation at all in that toe."

What made it almost supernatural, Roger Leir has explained, was that the area where he was probing has no tactile or pain receptors because it's deep inside muscle tissue. The body just doesn't grow tactile pain receptors there. Pain receptors that would have reacted are on and near the surface of the skin, especially in the foot, which has to be sensitive to anything that can cause injury. That's why stepping with your bare feet on rough surfaces—pebbles, shells in the water, hot sand, splintery wooden boardwalks, and the like—causes such incredible discomfort. However, deep beneath the surface of the skin, where the woman's melon seed object was located, there are no pain receptors. No pain receptors, no way for the woman to have felt pain. Yet when Leir touched the object with the edge of the probe to position it for extraction, it created such a wave of pain that the operation had to be stopped and the patient reanesthetized and put back into a deep hypnotic state before the operation could be resumed.

This time Roger Leir managed to reach the object

and extract it. He knew the patient was feeling some sensation, even though they thoroughly tested the surface of the patient's foot to make sure she had no feeling. But he was able to complete both extractions despite his patient's discomfort. And that's when he encountered the next stunning surprise.

He'd already been amazed to find that the woman had no entry wound or scars from where the objects should have entered her toe. Nor did Leir find any damage to the tissue under the skin where the objects would have to have traveled to get that deep into the toe, or evidence that the woman's body had tried to reject the object. How can a foreign object, obviously some sort of metal, lodge deep within human tissue without any evidence that the body had tried to reject it? It was as if the object had become part of the tissue where it was embedded. He'd also found that the woman seemed to have pain receptors in a place where normally there would be no pain receptors.

However, he discovered as he extracted the object, there was a very valid reason for the patient's pain reaction. The object he removed was encased in what seemed to be some kind of neural package. In fact, the patient's own neural tissue was used as a coating around the object, not only to encase it and protect it from a natural rejection, but to connect it, it seemed, to the rest of the woman's nervous system. It was as if the object were a kind of phone tap tied into the rest of the woman's neural network. Maybe he was crazy, Leir said to himself as he looked at the tough, black membrane he had extracted, but this wasn't something that occurred naturally around a foreign object. It looked as if someone, or something, had fabricated it out of the patient's own neural tissue. But it got worse. Dr. Leir discovered after analyzing the membrane that it had been formed out of the patient's surface nerve tissue, called superficial tissue. In other words, this was a type of surface skin tissue that doesn't form inside muscle tissue. There's no way the body can grow skin inside itself. Leir was looking at something way beyond weird; this had progressed into deeply disturbing.

The nature of the neural package around the foreign object also explained why the patient's body didn't reject the piece of metal—it probably didn't come into direct contact with it. If Dr. Leir was looking at a piece of bioengineering, which a very firm voice inside his brain was telling him he was, then it made perfect sense. Whatever caused this anomaly had packaged this metal object in the patient's body's own tissue, probably at the point of implantation, so that the body wouldn't recognize it as a foreign object. But the package, because it was made of surface nerve tissue, plugged directly into the patient's neural network. That made it resistant to any tampering while at the same time providing a seamless connection to whatever data were carried along the patient's neural net. In other words, it was hard-wired in.

Dr. Leir realized he was looking at a terrifyingly efficient way of capturing biological and informational data from a patient while protecting the capture device from the host's natural protective rejection mechanism. Everything about this metallic object defied standard medical knowledge. Dr. Leir, although fascinated at what was magnetically affixed to the end of his surgical instruments, didn't like what his medical instincts were telling him.

Let's say, Leir thought to himself as he looked down at the object, that this were some sort of device. Maybe it's an electronic tag; maybe it's something far more sinister. But whatever it is, the first question you'd have to ask is, Where's the power supply? There was no battery, no little generator, but there was a highly charged magnetic field around the object. Once he was able to pry it out of the package of neural membrane surrounding it, the thing absolutely clung to the edge of his scalpel. Leir ran a stud finder over the piece of metal and was amazed that the probe on the stud finder stood right on its end whenever he passed it over the metal. Could its magnetically charged field resonate with the patient's own low-level electrical field and somehow power itself? Could it draw its power from the patient, creating a unique electrical signature that made the abductee easy to locate while at the same time performing other functions? And what might these functions be?

The second object Dr. Leir removed from the woman was also packaged within a neural membrane that reacted when he touched it with his probe. But as Derrel Sims kept reinforcing the chemical anesthetic with suggestions that kept the patient as relaxed as possible, Roger Leir was able to remove the T-shaped piece of metal and close the wound without causing her additional discomfort. And then he peeled away the neural membrane and placed the second object on a piece of gauze next to the seed-shaped implant where he could compare them to one another.

A strange thing about the objects Dr. Leir noticed was

that they were smaller once removed from the neural packages than they appeared on the X rays. Could they have shrunk upon exposure to the air? Leir replaced one of the objects inside the neural package and it seemed to expand. This defied what Leir knew about the properties of metallic objects, but he didn't question what his own eyes were telling him. Whatever these things were, an analysis of their components would tell Leir and Sims a lot more than they knew standing alongside the patient.

The objects themselves were tough, standing up to any attempts to break them apart. The T-shaped object, particularly, wouldn't separate. So Leir and Sims packaged them in the patients' blood serum and had them sent off to a research facility in New Mexico for testing.

Leir didn't tell the analysts in New Mexico where the objects came from, he didn't dare. He only asked them what these things were made of and what, if any, conclusions might be drawn from an analysis of their composition.

The New Mexico laboratory performed extensive tests on the metal objects, including scanning electron microscopy, X-ray spectroscopy, and a complete analysis of the objects' chemical components. There were no strange or unusual elements, simply traces of copper, sodium, chlorine, and a magnetic iron core.

What was astonishing was the scientists' suggestions about the material they'd analyzed. Not knowing where Dr. Leir had gotten the objects, they asked if they came from a fallen meteor. "Why?" Leir asked. Because, they answered, the objects seemed to be made of meteoric material. In other words, the objects had an extraterrestrial origin. When Leir told the scientists that he had extracted them from the toe of one of his patients and the thumb of another patient, the scientists told him that he'd made a mistake. He'd mixed up the objects with something else, they suggested, because these couldn't possibly have come out of someone's body. They came from space.

Roger Leir knew, however, that the extraterrestrial nature of the composition of these objects meant that the patients truly must have had unusual experiences. "After all," Leir told interviewers who had asked him about the patients and the operations he'd performed. "This woman couldn't have stepped on a meteor. And if she did, how come there was no entry wound or other inflammation?"

When you put everything together, Leir realized, the evidence of something was there. But one's mind resisted believing that aliens in extraterrestrial spaceships were abducting humans and implanting them with strange devices. In subsequent operations over following years, Leir encountered objects very similar to the ones he removed from his first two patients. All of his extractions involved extra heavy doses of anesthesia when patients reacted to the probe, and in these cases Leir routinely found the implant enveloped in a sac of the patient's neural tissue. The metallic objects all seemed to have an extremely magnetic iron core, and patients seem to react to the removal of the object with a sense of loss.

One woman reported that it was as if another sense, akin to her other five senses, had been lost. She couldn't put her finger on what kind of perception the implant seemed to give her, but it was like an intuition, an awareness that she was part of something else. A man who'd carried his implant inside for many years actually mourned its loss. He said that a part of his personality was now gone, a part of *him,* as if someone else were living inside him and had abandoned him. And, in fact, abandonment was one of the psychological reactions patients seemed to express. Even those individuals who had expressed outrage at the invasiveness of the implants and said they felt as if they'd been victims of an assault because of what their abductors did, nevertheless reported experiencing various degrees of loss when the implants were finally removed. And still others claimed to have had subsequent encounters with an alien presence in which the aliens sought a form of revenge or punishment for the implant's removal.

Clearly, Dr. Leir thought, the nature of the connection between these implants of extraterrestrial material and reports of having been abducted needed to be explored. There was some real science here, Leir believed, but the reluctance of the scientific community to define it and evaluate its significance was frustrating. And, Leir discovered, there was also a great reluctance on the part of the medical community to engage in any formal study of the objects that Leir had removed. From where he had started, a workaday podiatric surgeon with a successful practice in one of Southern California's complacent residential communities, he now realized he had taken steps very close to the edge of reality and was peering into a frightening chasm whose implications he very reluctantly allowed himself to consider.

Implications

There are very compelling issues surrounding alien implants, whose existence, if true, may have profoundly disturbing implications. First there is the notion of implanted tracking devices, which in itself is part of our own technology. We use tracking devices in all sorts of agricultural industries to keep track of stock, monitor breeding patterns, and manage inventory. In fact, as Richard Sauder has written in *UFO Magazine,* a patent for an inserted transponder device granted to Destron Fearing, Inc., specifically states that not only is the device, in this case a transponder, to be embedded in the animal to be identified, but that "the primary object of this invention is to provide a system for identifying an object, animal, or person." Data from the transponder or tracking device can be relayed to a compatible computer system for data storage and management.

As a benign system for managing a herd of cows or pigs, this type of monitoring system is almost innocuous. But, as Sauder speculates, there is nothing in this system that prevents it from tracking human beings. The same devices that insert tiny transponders into the ear of a pig can just as easily insert it into the nasal passage or toe of a human being. If, as the product has been advertised, the system can manage the data of a population of 34 billion units, be they people or livestock, the implications become downright sinister. Imagine just such a system used for some form of social management on a scale so large it simply escapes our attention. Are we in the testing stages of just such a program and are alien abductions simply a screen—a convenient screen—for a truly Draconian program of human control through implanted devices? Remember, if a powerful enough entity, even if it's a private company, has the technology and the resources, it might not necessarily seek government permission to carry out a program. And if the group is under contract to one of the intelligence agencies in a social experiment, experiments like MK ULTRA, which the CIA has admitted to in the past, you won't necessarily find the story on the front page of your local newspaper until it's all over.

On the other hand, what if these are alien abductions and some race, whether malevolent or not, is tracking us either for breeding purposes or as part of some information-gathering scheme to serve their own purposes? We are to them as herds of farm animals are to us. Then these tracking devices, perhaps identifiable from spacecraft at great distances by a unique magnetic resonance, might make sense even if we don't like it or can't do anything about it. But, as some researchers have said, there's also the possibility that these implants do far more than simply identify someone's location. Because they seem to be tied into the abductee's nervous system, what if they're also two-way monitoring devices. The abductee, or implantee, in this case, is not only tracked, but what the individual sees and hears is picked up just as operatives in an undercover intelligence-gathering operation can pick up a conversation from a listening device planted in a hotel room. And it's two-way.

Those individuals who report that somehow they feel another presence inside them, a presence that's no longer there once the implant is removed, might not just be reporting a psychological symptom. They might be reporting a very real presence implanted by the nature of the device itself. Married through a membrane of dense nerve tissue into the individual's own neural system, the device may actually be transmitting a very low level of electrical signals into areas of the person's brain to stimulate it as well as monitor it. Of course there's another presence, there's a constant two-way transmission going on between those who implanted the device and the individual. Does this mean that alien monitors sit at screens in a spaceship just outside Earth's atmosphere telling us when to eat a pizza slice or grab a cup of coffee? Probably not. But if there were a set of software instructions unique to the implant, set to a pattern routine for the individual which could be modified from abduction to abduction, it would be almost completely cybernetic, turning individual abductees into monitoring devices as well as operatives. And that would be a level of extraterrestrial intervention even more frightening than most people can contemplate.

The Alternatives

If we assume that the implants discovered by abductees and removed by Roger Leir are not extraterrestrial at all but simply the results of accidents, pieces of debris that people stepped on, we still run up against the medical anomalies that Leir discovered during the operations. How can we account for the neural package, the lack of an entry wound, inflammation, or the body's failure to reject the foreign object? Dr. Leir couldn't, and that's what led him to believe there was something completely abnormal about the implants he discovered.

But we also know that we have the current commercial-level technology, and have had for at least the past decade or so, to implant devices capable of tracking, monitoring, and relaying data about the implantee to a larger database. This might enable intelligence organizations or companies under contract to intelligence organizations to conduct their own experiments, albeit with a sampling of subjects, in population monitoring or control. How realistic is this scenario?

Unfortunately, if these implants, alien or not, are a real phenomenon, which Dr. Leir's research seems to suggest is true, then we are left with a possibility of two very unpleasant alternatives. Either the enemy is an alien presence of some type that is using individuals as part of a control strategy or experiment in species management or perhaps hybridization of a new species, or the enemy is within our own governments. While an alien presence is certainly staggering to the imagination, the possibility that we're doing this to ourselves is perhaps even more sinister. Or maybe, just maybe, parts of our own government are working for an alien presence and with their assistance are monitoring the program for them. These are all thoroughly disturbing possibilities that carry with them dark and potentially terrifying implications.

Part of us wants to believe that either somehow Roger Leir is mistaken or there are completely typical explanations for the objects he's extracted. But if those explanations are provided, will they only lull us into a false sense of security? Maybe the very existence of objects implanted in people who've claimed an abduction experience should be the kind of alarm that tells us something is very wrong out there in the darkness where we can't see but where completely self-serving organizations may be hard at work. And if this means some entity, either on this planet or elsewhere, is planning its own version of a future for us, maybe other medical doctors and scientists should take a closer and more open-minded look at the work of Roger Leir, Whitley Streiber, Budd Hopkins, John Mack, David Jacobs, Yvonne Smith, and others, who listen to what abductees have to say and listen without prejudice or scorn.

CHAPTER 7

The Screaming Alien

"I [have] every confidence that the American public would be able to take such information without hysteria. The fear of the unknown is always greater than fear of the known."

Representative Walter H. Moeller, Ohio

THERE HAVE BEEN MANY REVELATIONS ABOUT UFO EN-counters on the nationally syndicated *Art Bell Show,* one of the most popular radio talk shows in America. One of the most intriguing stories by far was related by psychologist Dr. Jonathan Reed about his encounter deep in the forests of Washington's Cascade Mountains.

Seattle psychologist Dr. Reed had taken his Golden Retriever, Suzy, with him for a hike on one of the Cascade Mountains trails, glad to be out of the city. It was October 1996, a glorious fall day, perfect for taking photos of deer, fox, or any other animals in the wild he might come across. That was why he'd packed cameras along with his gear when he set out that morning, he told Art Bell in a 1998 radio interview. It was exercise as much for his dog as for himself because in Seattle there weren't many places were dogs could run around free. On the northwest trails of the Cascades, there was room for his dog to run, plenty of solitude, and maybe something interesting to photograph.

It was about three in the afternoon as Suzy bounded ahead of her master, enthusiastically enjoying a world of wonderful animal scents and exploring everything in her path. In and out of thickets she leaped, sniffing the base of every tree and investigating everything she could get her nose into. Suddenly, something up ahead caught her attention and she simply took off after whatever it was. Maybe she smelled a rabbit, Jonathan Reed thought, or another animal. And that's when the loud barking started.

At first it was the normal barking of a dog that had made a discovery and was barking to intimidate something, establish its territory, or signal to the pack. Then the barking changed. It became more menacing, as if what had been discovery had turned to anger. This was now a confrontation; the dog was in a fight. Maybe this was a really large animal, Dr. Reed thought. They'd seen a bear earlier that day, and if the dog had cornered a bear or a bear cornered the dog, then there really would be a fight unless he could scare the animal away. So Jonathan Reed grabbed a hefty tree branch that he could wield like a club or a baseball bat if he needed to, and started off after the sound of his dog's barking.

Suzy had disappeared into the forest, possibly a hundred fifty yards ahead of him, he told the national radio audience, so he had no idea what was going on amid the dense trees. However, he could hear that his dog's barking had changed again. Now, intermixed with the defensive growling were the yelps of a dog in the middle of a fight. There was fear here, he thought, something was threatening his dog's life. That's when he climbed up to a small ridge and saw Suzy in a clearing being attacked, it looked like, by something that was moving at a furious speed and vibrating so quickly it seemed to be in many places at once. This was no animal, he thought, it was something else. And it was moving at a speed fast enough to be a blur in his vision as it moved back and forth, stirring up the air around the dog. It was like nothing Dr. Reed had seen in his life. What could move that fast, so fast you couldn't tell precisely where it stood at any moment?

Suddenly the thing reached out from inside the blur and grabbed the dog's snout, while at the same time the dog got its jaws around the thing's forearm. Dr. Reed, now caught up in the emotion of a life-and-death struggle between his retriever and some humanoid thing he couldn't identify, yelled at Suzy to release the forearm and get back. But it was too late, the thing looked like it was tearing the dog's head back, ripping it right off its body. Then it stopped moving—stopped "vibrating" was how Dr. Reed described it—and looked at Reed with a stare that seemed actually murderous. It turned back to the dog, pulled the flesh off its skull, then tore back its skull, and Jonathan Reed watched as the animal began to die. He could see that the entire head had been torn back from the jaw, which was now completely exposed, to the animal's neck. It was a frightening sight to look at all the exposed bone as the animal began, in the words of Robert Raith—a confidant of Jonathan Reed's and a guest on Art Bell's radio show that night— "to implode into itself." It looked like something inside the animal was sucking the dog's mass into some central core of nothingness. Suzy seemed to be absorbed into a black hole, leaving only white ash in a small pile on the ground.

Now Dr. Reed lunged after the creature, who had turned its attention toward him. It was no longer vibrating now, but was standing still. It took a step backward and looked at Reed, probably in preparation for another attack. Acting out of what he believed to be a fear for his own life, Reed sized the creature up and got ready to lunge.

In the moments before he struck, Reed noticed that this thing—he was now calling it an alien—was as small as a child. But it was no child, at least not a child from this planet, he thought. It was about four-and-a-half feet tall, able to take steps like a human being, but also capable of moving incredibly fast. It had large bloated eyes, which it was able to open and close, but they were a light color, not the dense black abductees have reported seeing on the creatures poised over them on the examination table. Then—maybe it was the way the creature got ready to move or even jump at him—Reed was suddenly seized by an immediate fear for his own life. He struck the creature over the head as hard as he could with his tree limb. The entity emitted a horrifying shriek that Reed said he could only describe as a scream, even though the word "scream" can't convey the terror in the sound of the creature's voice. And as it screamed, it fell to the ground and stopped moving.

Reed looked down and could see that his blow, wielded as if he were swinging a baseball bat, had ripped open a hole in the creature's skull to expose a deep red gushing wound. It had cracked an outer mantle of what Reed believed was the creature's cranium and exposed some tissue underneath the bone. The creature was lying on the soft ground amid leaves, completely motionless except for the red ooze slowly coming out of the wound. To Dr. Reed, staring at the alien life-form on the ground that had just killed his dog with its bare hands, what had happened was an episode of madness and horror. He went into what he described as a state of shock.

He simply stared at the thing on the ground, thinking at first that maybe it was a child after all, perhaps wearing some king of bizarre Halloween costume that he was trying out for the end of the month. Part of his fear was that he, a practicing psychologist and now a research psychologist, had committed some kind of violent crime. But, as he stared, he realized that this thing was not human. It was not a human child in some strange costume wearing an alien mask but a different kind of life-form: humanoid, certainly, human in shape, but not human as we understand the word. The head was angular and pointed and didn't have human facial expressions. The creature was wearing what appeared to be a one-piece black outer garment that was so tight, it covered every part of its body from its head to its feet without any obvious seam.

Fear was washing over Jonathan Reed, consuming his every thought. What was he really staring at as he analyzed the thing on the ground? What had he just clubbed with the tree limb in an act of violence that he would have thought himself incapable of performing just fifteen minutes earlier? He had to sit down. He simply collapsed in a heap a few feet away from the motionless body and waited for his strength to return. Perhaps he should see to his dog, he thought, and tried to regain his feet, but he lost his balance and fell forward, completely overcome with dizziness and nausea.

Dr. Reed could recognize the symptoms of physical and traumatic shock. And he hoped that by remaining on the ground and waiting for the waves of nausea and terror to pass over him he would ultimately be able to get back to his feet and take stock of the situation. He knew that his car was perhaps an hour or so back down the trail and that he had to get some sort of record of this situation. So he waited for another hour, forcing his mind to focus on the immediate situation and how he could collect the emotional strength to get back on his feet.

That's when he took the first photographs of the strange being. He wanted to record the event while he still had enough light amid the shadows of the tall trees to get a clear image. He was barely functional, he remembers, wracked in emotional turmoil because of the sudden violence, the destruction of his dog, and the absolute fear that whatever killed his dog would come after him next. What Dr. Reed did, he said, was instinctive, yet his job as a psychologist was to mediate violence away, to prevent it from taking place. He had just struck back out of raw fear and performed an act that his professional training told him he should prevent. And that's what was causing his mind to blur and his body to go weak every time he realized what he'd done.

As far as he was concerned, life as he knew it had fallen apart around him. He was overwhelmed with guilt because he'd killed something. Every time he felt the strength return to his legs he walked over to it again. He had to make sure that the creature didn't turn into a child. Maybe the whole event was a hallucination and it really was a child lying there. Part of him even hoped that it was human, no matter what, because the alternative was that he'd just fought a pitched battle with something that was not supposed to exist. He wanted to turn away from the horror even as he forced himself to stare at the creature and to take the photos, because no one would believe his story without proof. He didn't even believe it, even still.

The Obelisk

After two more hours of emotional turmoil during which Dr. Reed tried to confront what had happened and what it meant, he noticed a strange humming in his ears. The shadows had lengthened and it would soon be dark, but he had to investigate. It was more than a sound, he remembered, almost like a presence, a part of which he could hear. He felt the presence, like a form of energy, brush against his skin as it approached, and his skin reacted with the kind of electrostatic tension that raises goose pimples and causes your hair to stand up. He could make out a direction to the sound, so he followed it. Maybe, he thought, he would find someone else nearby who might be able to help him. But, even though he was hoping against hope that it was another hiker out there whose presence he felt, it turned out to be something else entirely.

First, Reed felt a wave from some kind of energy

field crash over him. He described the feeling of being surrounded by static electricity. It was so intense, he tried to run back the way he'd come, but his legs were too weak to carry him and he fell. As he tried to roll over and get back to his feet, his knees went weak and he got sick again. With his stomach knotted up from nausea and his muscles weak from shock and from whatever energy was surrounding him, Reed tried to struggle to his feet and locate the presence that was affecting him. If he couldn't outrun it, maybe he could outflank it. But he didn't know what the "it" was.

Through the bushes, he could see something moving, although he couldn't identify it. Then he moved toward it, and now saw something floating in the air. It was black, hard-angled, and had a tower with a point rising about two or so feet out of it that made Dr. Reed think it looked like a small obelisk. That's what he called it to himself, an obelisk, while trying to snap off a photo or two. But because the air was so heavy with static electricity he didn't know whether the camera would work.

The strange object frightened him, although it took no hostile action at first. He backed away again, still trying to take pictures without exposing himself should it fire some kind of weapon at him. All the while he felt enveloped in an energy field that he hoped against hope wasn't a radiation field that was slowly poisoning him. But as the obelisk simply hung in the air and took no action, Dr. Reed had the odd feeling that he could approach it.

With his camera poised to keep taking pictures, Dr. Reed slowly made his way back toward the humming object. He felt as though he were walking through a gauzy web of electricity. The humming continued, but Dr. Reed kept walking until he was right next to it. It extended to almost ten feet, with a width of about four feet. The dimensions of this thing seemed odd to him, unaerodynamic almost. But it didn't move as he walked up. Then he put out his hand and touched it. The humming stopped.

The object was as hard as stone, Dr. Reed told Art Bell's radio audience, and very cold. It was like touching ice. He removed his hand and the humming started up again, only this time it seemed to be a more friendly sound. Was this a form of communication?

Jonathan Reed reached out to touch it one more time, but he lost his balance on the slippery ground. And as he tried to catch himself, his other hand hit the object with a hard slap. To his surprise, there was no sound at all when his hand hit it, and the object didn't even move. It just hung there, hovering about three-and-a-half feet in the air. He felt his hand begin to tingle, then burn in exactly the spot where he had touched the object. And he continued to feel ill as the effects of the energy field kept working on him. He didn't know whether he'd been exposed to radiation or whether the electrostatic field was making him weaker. So, as the sky began to grow dark, Dr. Reed decided it was time to get out of there. Maybe his life would return to reality if he could put all this behind him. There was just one problem: the dead alien on the ground.

At first, Jonathan Reed said he wanted to bury it. But he didn't have a shovel with him, so he figured maybe he'd scratch out a small hollow in the ground with the pocket knife he had and cover it with the thermo blanket he'd packed, then come back later with help. No sense trying to dig a hole without a shovel. But all the rocks in the area were buried so deep that it would take forever, and probably require a shovel. He rolled the creature onto his thermo blanket. But the creature was so easy to handle, he figured it must have weighed only fifty pounds or so. It was as if it were a hollow mannequin. He lifted it, hefted it, and realized that he could carry it back down the trail and throw it in the trunk of his car. Better that, he said to himself, than have someone discover the body in the woods and walk away with what might be one of the most astonishing finds in the history of humankind.

Stopping every now and then to rest and take the load off his shoulder, Dr. Reed carried the creature rolled up in the blanket back down the trail for about ninety minutes. He thought about hiding it somewhere in the bushes or thickets, but decided to keep on going. He reached the car, opened the trunk, dropped the creature in, and slammed the lid shut. Then he took a breath, and for a moment felt as if he were in control once again. But he knew it was an illusion because images of the two strange encounters he had had were playing like a videotape loop inside his mind. Then there was the physical presence of the dead creature he'd just tossed into his trunk, and the terrifying memory of his dog dissolving into a mound of ash on the ground. No, this wasn't the reality he'd expected to find when he decided to go hiking.

Jonathan Reed didn't waste any time. He drove straight home to Seattle, welcoming his return to the real world of the city. Sitting in his car outside his garage, he told his audience, he realized that he had to figure out what to do with the alien. Where was he going to bury it? Then he realized he actually only needed to preserve it. After all, it was the only real physical evidence he had besides the photos and the video. He knew he couldn't leave it in the car, so he put the body in the meat freezer in the garage. At least that way, he thought, he'd keep it under lock and key while at the same time he preserved the flesh. He still didn't know whether he was going to bury it or not, but he wanted to put everything behind him as much as possible while he figured out his next move.

After he'd slammed the freezer door shut, Dr. Reed could almost believe that he'd closed the door on a nightmare. Maybe, when he came back the next morning, the body would be gone and he could forget about the whole thing. But, the next morning when he came to check, sure enough, the thing was in there, and he knew he had to photograph it. He set up his video camera right next to the freezer by duct-taping it to a ladder, opened the door and removed the alien bundle still wrapped in the outdoor blanket, and unrolled the bundle across the floor. Then, documented in an astounding video which Art Bell described live on the air, Dr. Reed began an examination—ghoulish according to anyone's characterization of it—in which he moved the creature's head back and forth, opened its mouth and eyelids, and manipulated its face.

He called a few friends, he said, because he wanted to share the stress of what had happened and show them what he had. But he was only able to reach one of his friends, an individual named Gary, who saw the creature and told him that they were probably looking at an alien. This was the last thing Dr. Reed wanted to hear from someone else, though it confirmed what he already believed, even from the first moments after he had clubbed the thing to death. What about calling the police? After all, whatever it was, Dr. Reed believed he had killed it. But Gary insisted the police were the last place they wanted to go. Besides, what could the police do: call the air force or, worse, the CIA? They were only putting themselves at risk. If the thing were really an alien, they should call UFO groups, large UFO groups, to get this creature investigated and analyzed by professionals and to put the results out there in the public arena where people would talk about it. That was the only way to protect themselves. They began with MU-FON, the Mutual UFO Network.

But if Dr. Reed thought that the UFO community could provide some aid or comfort in this devastating situation, he quickly learned otherwise. He remarked that some of the groups wanted to tear the creature apart like a piece of meat to see what made the thing tick, as well as put Dr. Reed's own life under a microscope. They acted as though Jonathan Reed were a threat instead of a victim. Something this good, this juicy, they said, couldn't be true.

Then Jonathan Reed tried talking to some of the professionals he knew in the research and university communities. But they were reluctant to become involved, and in fact, when Dr. Reed told them what had happened, some of them became downright scared. Only one person, a professor at a local university, seemed excited by what Reed had to say. He planned to come over to take a look at the thing himself, he said. Then, hours later, the professor called back and said that he had to cancel their meeting. He wouldn't be coming after all, he admitted reluctantly, seeming very frightened.

One after the other, all the people Reed had called told him they weren't going to get involved. Reed was beginning to feel that he was all alone in this, alone with a dead alien in his freezer. And that was when he realized he actually wasn't alone at all. There were people watching his house.

It began with a feeling that he and his friend Gary were being followed wherever they went. It was as if someone were tapping Reed's phone and knew whenever he had plans to leave. Then Reed began seeing a dark blue van wherever he went. But his paranoia at seeing a dark vehicle following him changed to panic when the van twice tried to run his car off the road. These incidents, combined with the cancellations of appointments with people who could help him examine the creature and give him some advice, made him feel that his life was actually in danger. And it wasn't something he could make go away, because he couldn't erase his encounter with the creature. He had seen something he was never supposed to see, and now he was going to be erased. Then he heard the thump in the freezer.

The Thing That Wouldn't Die

He was in the garage when he first heard the sound. He was putting away the examination table where he had planned to videotape the alien when the *thump, thump, thump* noise started from underneath the freezer. Probably just the motor, Reed thought, but what a lousy time for the motor to go out. What if he had to contend with a rotting alien? Just in case, he'd have to empty the freezer and get someone out to replace the compressor. But maybe he could check it out first. Reed crawled around the unit to inspect the motor, but found it was working perfectly. Maybe it was an animal that had crawled underneath, got itself trapped, and was working its way out. Maybe it was a rat. But there were no rats behind the unit, and he couldn't find any other animal. And the sounds wouldn't stop no matter what he did. Then he realized they were coming from inside the freezer.

Slowly, Dr. Reed opened the freezer door to see what could possibly be making the thumping sound—and that's when he saw the alien move. It shook inside its blanket. And then, while Dr. Reed's blood almost turned to ice as he stared down into the freezer, the alien screamed.

He slammed down the freezer door and ran back into the house.

What had happened? Jonathan Reed said later that when he checked on the torn tissue around the head wound on one of the times he had taken the alien out of the freezer, he noticed that the tissue that had been torn away from the bone was now adhering to it. Perhaps the alien was healing. Clearly neither the diminished oxygen atmosphere nor the subfreezing temperatures hurt the alien in any way. Perhaps they even helped the tissue heal and were somehow instrumental in the alien's coming back to life. Whatever the case, Jonathan Reed now had an alien in the freezer who was alive and thumping. It was squirming around, but very slowly, seemingly struggling against its injuries. But it was still alive. It was too weak to pose any threat, Dr. Reed thought, so he continued examining the creature and capturing the creature's movements on video. He also decided to try some experiments on the creature's outer garment.

The Outer Garment

Dr. Reed didn't know whether the creature's skintight covering was a kind of environmental suit, a space suit, or part of the creature itself. There was only one real way to check and that was to try to remove the garment, or if he couldn't find a fastener, to cut it away. And that's exactly what he tried to do while documenting the operation to remove the clothing.

The clothing—if that's what it can even be called— was almost like a protective "skin" that generated a defensive force field, Dr. Reed found. He explained in the Art Bell interview that when he first tried to cut an incision in the alien's clothing, the material seemed to liquefy around the blade he was using and rejoin with itself. It was like cutting through a thin gelatin. When he tried it again the same thing happened even though he tried a longer cut. The material simply turned into a kind of gel and re-formed as the knife blade passed through it. Finally, on the third time, the liquid gel seemed to bond with the knife blade, adhering to the cutting edge so the knife couldn't even penetrate. All of this was on a video-tape that, Dr. Reed explained, went missing when the people who were surveilling him ransacked his house.

The Search and Seizure

Friends of Dr. Reed had told him that they were being watched by strange people. They reported that they thought their houses had been searched and that people were following them. Dr. Reed, over the week or so that he'd kept the alien, had been using some of his friends' houses to hide his film and videos of the alien and had begun to feel that these locations were no longer safe. So he began to retrieve his pictures and materials and to move them around so that if photos were seized—whether by the military or the government—he would at least have some of the material left. Finally, on the ninth day following Dr. Reed's capture of the alien, he returned home to see strange vans in his driveway. There were people in his house, so he kept on driving as if he didn't know the place and hoped no one was following him.

When he returned a day later, he found that the house had been broken into and turned inside out. Pieces of furniture lay everywhere. There was not much left of anything he owned, Dr. Reed could see as he looked around the devastation the intruders had wreaked. There were holes in his floor where floorboards had been pulled right off the joists, holes in the ceiling where someone had pulled down great chunks to see if anything was hidden up there, and holes in the walls as well. They had gone through every inch of space and everything he owned. This was not a methodical search, but a desperate, frantic hunt. They didn't care what they broke or destroyed. They wanted something and would have destroyed anything that stood in their way. And by the time Dr. Reed got to the garage to see what they'd done, he knew that they had found what they wanted. The alien was gone.

They had taken every piece of evidence of his encounter with the alien. In the garage he found that the door had been ripped completely off its hinges, broken into pieces, and cast to the side of the structure. Inside, the garage had been ransacked and the freezer carted away. Dr. Reed was devastated. This, he believed, had been an act of the authorities, probably in order to remove the incontrovertible evidence of a secret they'd worked hard to protect for at least fifty years. There were no police he could call, no federal agencies there to protect any of his rights, no friends in high circles to whom he could turn.

Gary, the person he'd called to help him photograph the alien, fled Seattle with him and then, separately, they went underground, moving from location to location, never staying in any one place long enough to be discovered. For two years Gary and Jonathan Reed traveled between cities along the West Coast from San Diego to Portland, remaining out of sight and contact. For all Dr. Reed knew, his friend had been arrested or kidnapped. Ultimately, when he did make contact with his friend in 1998, Dr. Reed said that it was as if something had changed. His friend was no longer forthcoming about what had happened to him or what his current condition was.

When Reed first realized that he was being followed in the days after he stashed the alien in his freezer and had begun shooting videos of the creature, he'd begun placing the videos with different friends for safekeeping. If the authorities raided his house, Reed thought, maybe he would be able to retrieve some of the pieces of his documentation from this group of friends, one of whom was a woman named Dolly. He'd left some very dramatic videos in her possession. Then he left Seattle, hiding out for about two months before daring to contact anyone in the group. When he thought it safe to emerge from hiding just long enough to try to retrieve some of his videos, he contacted Dolly to let her know that he was on his way.

But when he got to her house days later, he found her dead body curled up on the floor. Careful not to disturb anything, he conducted a quick search for his video, but it was nowhere to be found. Dolly was dead; his materials were gone. And although Dolly's death certificate lists heart attack as the cause of death, her relationship to the screaming alien materials and to Jonathan Reed leaves him very suspicious about what really might have happened.

All that was left to him was to hold on to the remaining photos and video and somehow get part of it into the hands of the public so that people could see his discovery. With the help of a small group of friends he could trust not to disclose his whereabouts, a group he nicknamed "The Alliance," and relying on radio programs such as the *Art Bell Show* where he believed he would get an open hearing, Dr. Reed went under-ground—this time for good, he believed—fleeing for his life from whatever agency was chasing him to silence his story about the screaming alien.

Is it a government agency on his trail, maybe the National Security Agency or the CIA, trying to keep him from disclosing critical information about an alien presence on planet Earth? Is it part of a military intelligence organization, a military unit that operates in this country to keep any firsthand evidence of an alien entity from getting out to the public? Dr. Reed can't answer this.

Many individuals who have seen Dr. Reed's photos believe his story without a doubt. There are others who will believe it to be a hoax until and unless it can be corroborated by the reappearance of the alien itself for some kind of independent testing. Certainly Dr. Reed's appearance on the *Art Bell Show* amazed and astonished the radio audience and the members of Art's guest panel, which included one of the most outspoken of public advocates for the abductee community, best-selling author Whitley Streiber. And until the results of whatever photo analysis and testing of the stills and videos that Dr. Reed shot is completed, all we have to go on is the firsthand witness report of Dr. Reed and the descriptions that whoever else handled the alien can give us. But, given the nature of the story and the photos, some of which are freely available at Dr. Reed's Web site and the Art Bell Web site (www.odysseylink.com and www.artbell.com), this might be one of the most astounding UFO encounters in recent history.

CHAPTER 8

The Far Side of the Moon

> *"I strongly recommend that there be a committee investigation of the UFO phenomena. I think we owe it to the people to establish credibility regarding UFOs and to produce the greatest possible enlightenment on this subject."*
>
> Congressman Gerald Ford, March 28, 1966

UFO MYSTERIES COME IN ALL KINDS OF PACKAGES. A few, like the Screaming Alien, represent someone's adventures in the world of the unknown. Others are more conventional—if that word can be used to describe UFO encounters—such as sighting of unexplained lights in the sky or strange objects floating in the distance. And still others have more to do with history and theory, or perhaps a chance brush against a fact or two that doesn't fit with traditional explanations, than an actual one-on-one alien encounter. It's in this last category that many people would place lunar transient phenomena, or LTP as they're sometimes called. Lunar transient phenomena consist of the anomalies that people, sometimes even our own NASA astronauts, have noticed in the vicinity of the moon. And these anomalies have spawned an area of

UFO studies fraught with the possibility that, for who knows how long, alien entities might have inhabited the moon or used it as a base for missions to Earth.

There are intriguing clues about the nature of the moon, among them strange sightings of lights, the avid interest the U.S. Army expressed in the 1950s to place a military base on the moon, the reports people say the Apollo astronauts made about strange structures and craft on the moon, and the photos of odd structures on the moon that some analysts say couldn't possibly be natural features. These clues could be indicators that there is much more about the moon and what our government knows than most of us can even begin to understand. Can something that all of us see just about every night and which we think we know so well really be an unsolved mystery after all these millennia?

Those who research and write about lunar anomalies point to lunar observation records going back over a hundred years in which scientists have claimed to have seen strange lights hovering over the lunar surface. Others assert that there are strange structures on the moon such as bridges, towers, and odd configurations of rock that could not have been the result of natural forces. And still others suggest that there is activity beneath the lunar surface that belies the scientific classification of the moon as geologically dead: that the moon is probably hollow and might well be the base for alien inhabitants.

And then there are the witnesses, the few individuals who by pure happenstance come into contact with just a little bit of evidence from the other side of reality that suggests, only for a split second but that's all it takes, that there is a hidden universe, a clandestine policy, and those in the know will kill to protect the great secret. That's what happened to Karl Wolfe one day, long before he began his career as a consulting producer for a local Los Angeles television station, while he was still a young technician in the United States Air Force during the premier Lunar Orbiter mission in 1965.

The Strange Photo from the Moon

Stationed at Langley Field, Virginia, with the 4444th Reconnaissance Technical Group at Headquarters Tactical Air Command, Airman Karl Wolfe worked for the director of intelligence. Langley Field was a data processing hub for the lunar orbiter project. The orbiter sent down all types of data to satellite receivers around the world, which were connected to Langley via land lines. At Langley, the data were converted to photographic images at a highly secure laboratory administered by NASA. Wolfe himself, he said during an interview at *UFO Magazine,* was one of only two technicians at the field who had the high-level security clearance to allow them to work with photo images from U-2s and surveillance satellites. This was at a time in the middle 1960s when most Americans had no knowledge of the extent of satellite surveillance and flights of U-2s, even though the Francis Gary Powers incident had made the world's newspaper headlines just four years earlier.

NASA equipment and the air force photo image enhancement equipment were quite similar, Wolfe recalls, similar enough that when a piece of NASA's equipment went down, the call went out to the air force reconnaissance group for help. As it happened that day, Wolfe was the only technician on the base with the training, knowledge, and expertise to repair that specific device. Accordingly, he was sent over to the NASA installation on the base to see if he could fix the equipment.

Karl Wolfe says he was driven over to the NASA hangar all the way on the other side of the base, where upon arrival he was granted a higher level of security clearance than the badge he was wearing indicated he had. It was a standard practice, he explained, when you entered areas that housed the most secret operations on the base. Wolfe says he was amazed at the types of people at work in the hangar. It was as if he had entered a different world.

All the separate work areas were sectioned off from each other by heavily draped black curtains. He noticed lots of scientists present, individuals wearing their photo security badges around their necks as they milled through the sections as if they were walking through the exhibition hall at a large convention. Who are all these people? he asked himself, people from all over the world, from what he could make out from their badges. He was amazed at the number of people from foreign countries with the security clearance to work on a base that was so shrouded in official secrecy. He was even more amazed that very few of them were speaking English. He recognized people speaking Japanese and German and even—this was during the cold war—Russian. He was truly overwhelmed at the sight.

The malfunctioning equipment that Karl Wolfe had been called to repair was in a darkroom which was staffed by a single airman working under a red safety light. Karl knew that he couldn't run the diagnostics on the photo enhancing printer as long as it was in the dark-room, and the effort would take some time. So he told the airman that the printer had to be removed from the darkroom. As they waited for personnel to arrive who would remove the equipment to a secure location, Wolfe asked the airman what the device was enhancing, and why, if it belonged to a NASA mission, it was here at Langley instead of at the space center in Houston.

The airman explained how all of the land lines from all the lunar orbiter downlinks around the world brought the data signals to Langley, where they were converted into photo strips that had to be assembled according to matching codes, then enhanced and printed. The prints were then sent to the scientists for analysis and inter-pretation. Without this device, the strips of film couldn't be converted into the large contact prints for evaluation. That was why it had to be repaired quickly.

But why all the security? Wolfe asked. And why was all the data coming here instead of Houston? And the airman began to explain in the small room, dark but for a small red light above them.

There was good reason for the security, he said. After all, he had seen some of the photos himself and had heard the conversations among the scientists about what they'd discovered on the side of the moon that was always pointed away from earth. "We discovered," the airman said in an almost matter-of-fact way, "a base on the back side of the moon." Karl Wolfe could only stammer in response. His whole body shivered as if he'd just walked through a door-way to another reality. "Yes," the airman continued, "a base on the other side of the moon." He didn't say whose it was, but Wolfe got the idea that it wasn't ours.

As if to emphasize his point, the airman laid down a bunch of newly enhanced photos directly under the small red bulb. Karl knew he was in dangerous territory, dangerous not only because he could very well be a dead man once he stepped out of that room if anybody knew he'd seen something he wasn't supposed to see, but dead to whatever innocence he possessed about the world as he knew it. Once you know what's really out there, your confidence in the basic assumptions of this world are no longer the same. So Karl looked down at the photos and saw an organization of geometric shapes and what looked to be, astonishingly enough, actual artificial structures. And in that moment he realized the reason why the international throng of scientists was milling about the hangar. They had been assembled to see this photo evidence of fabricated structures on the moon. But whose were they?

As Karl Wolfe describes them, at least one of the structures seemed to have circular antennas that reminded him of an array of radar antennas. It surprised him, because although they could have been alien in nature, why would aliens have radar antennas unless the aliens were very much like us. There was also the possibility that this could have been a joint Earth/alien base—especially because Karl Wolfe had the feeling that the international group of scientists in attendance at the hangar weren't really all human. It was as if there were an alien presence, an extraterrestrial presence, among the group. But it was only a feeling, and Wolfe dismissed it as being irrational and without foundation. He had his job to perform, a rigorous, tedious diagnostic of the contact printer which, as a result of what was being downloaded from the land lines running into Langley, was probably one of the most important pieces of equipment on the base.

Over the next two days, Karl Wolfe returned to the facility to troubleshoot each component in the photo enhancer until he gradually replaced all of the faulty relays and component circuits and the device was working again. And although for thirty years Wolfe tried to put the incident out of his memory, it would return to haunt him time and again. Because he had a high-level security clearance, he was not allowed to leave the country for the five years after his discharge from the air force without permission from the State Department, not even to jump across the New York State border from Buffalo into Canada.

The strange photos he saw told him that there was some sort of activity on the dark side of the moon, away from the prying eyes of Earthbound astronomers and their telescopes. Whether these were part of an alien base, erected by extraterrestrials for their own purposes, or a joint alien/human military base, he couldn't tell. The circular radar antennas looked to be part of a completely normal military base, photos of which he'd seen in satellite surveillance images and in U-2 images throughout his career in the air force. Yet the year was 1965, a full four years before any NASA astronaut would officially set foot on the lunar surface. So what were these images?

The Trudeau Files and Project Horizon

Buried away in army records so securely that not even former astronaut and retired United States Senator John Glenn knew of their existence are a series of once classified documents belonging to an army program called Project Horizon. Originally conceived as early as 1956, Project Horizon proposed the creation of an entirely new army command composed of elements from the Signal Corps, Artillery, the Medical Corps, the Army Corps of Engineers, and other units assembled for one purpose: to place a United States Army military base on the moon within the ensuing five or so years. Championed in 1959 by Lieutenant General Arthur Trudeau, the Director of Army Research and Development and former commander of Army Intelligence (G-2), Project Horizon argued the necessity of the army reaching the moon before the Soviets or any other hostile foreign power could seize the ultimate high ground.

There is an urgency to what General Trudeau is writing, almost a bugle call. The general—who was best known for charging up Pork Chop Hill during the Korean War when some of his men were trapped under heavy North Korean mortar fire—was attempting to marshal support for a monumental bureaucratic, logistic, and technological undertaking. Two years before President Kennedy's 1961 pledge to land human beings on the moon before the end of the 1960s, Trudeau was not asking for a mere landing, he was asking for a military fortification.

Project Horizon, now fully declassified, speaks for itself in descriptions, technical specifications, and logistics. However, the eloquence of Arthur Trudeau in describing the moon as the next potential battleground if the United States allowed the Soviets to gain the first territorial foothold there reminds one of the colonial wars when Britain and France were vying for supremacy in the New World. In explaining the degree of urgency, Trudeau argues:

> To be second to the Soviet Union in establishing an outpost on the moon would be disastrous to our nation's prestige and in turn to our democratic philosophy. Although it is contrary to United States policy, the Soviet Union in establishing the first permanent base, may claim the moon to or critical areas thereof for its own. Then a subsequent attempt to establish an outpost by the United States might be considered and propagandized as a hostile act. The Soviet Union in propaganda broadcasts has announced the 50th anniversary of the present government [1967] will be celebrated by Soviet citizens on the moon. The National Space policy intelligence estimate is that the Soviets could land on the moon by 1968.

Obviously, both the United States and the Soviet Union considered the moon a valuable military objective. But were we really only competing against one another? Was there another war going on that nobody inside government was talking about? Had a cold war with extraterrestrials already begun?

In the fifteen or so Apollo missions to the moon, little was said about the military advantage the United States was achieving against the Soviet Union during the final decade of the cold war, and there were no visible attempts to establish a manned military fortification or a permanent fortress on the lunar surface. But, what if what Karl Wolfe saw in photos when he was at Langley in 1965 represented someone else's—possibly an extraterrestrial—military communications presence on the moon? Perhaps that was behind General Trudeau's 1959 message to the Army Chief of the General Staff and to the Secretary of Defense and his support of Project Horizon. According to Colonel Philip Corso, General Trudeau belonged to a small cadre of senior military officers who were aware of an alien presence in our skies and in our solar system and were preparing for a coming conflict under the convenient aegis of the cold war with the Soviet Union.

Perhaps the lunar structures, the communications tower, that Karl Wolfe saw in 1965 either represented a secret United States unmanned lunar communications facility to monitor the Soviets or a Soviet facility designed to monitor us. Or perhaps the structure in the photograph that Wolfe saw was not designed to monitor either of the cold war superpowers but a venture on the part of one of the powers to monitor UFOs and their alien inhabitants, resulting from just the type of concentrated effort Trudeau was proposing back in 1959 in Project Horizon. As fantastic as it may seem, if what Karl Wolfe said he saw in the top secret photos is accurate, it is more believable to assume that the communications tower is human in origin rather than alien in origin and that monitoring an opposing superpower on Earth was a secondary mission rather than the primary one. If that's the case then it would mean there was a secret developmental curve that was far ahead, and probably still is, of the announced technology that is brought to bear. And if the mission were to spy on aliens from outer space, then the existence of the communications tower would probably still be a top state secret.

We do know that Project Horizon was officially turned down by the Eisenhower administration, because NASA took over the space exploration and moon launch program. General Trudeau lamented years later in his private memoirs that it had been one of his most important objectives. He wrote:

> Since 1957 we've seen the race for space go on, and I must say that one of the papers I'm breaking loose shortly is "Project Horizon." . . . When I was Chief of Research and Development it was apparent to me, as I've stated before, that there were military implications in space, and that the exploration, and perhaps even—I won't say occupation, but let's say residence—temporary residence on the moon would be important. Between the Ordnance and the Engineers, I directed them to come up with a plan for landing and living on the moon, and this carried at least as far as the Russians have gone today with their lunar vehicle. In other words, we designed a comprehensive program. When it was submitted to me and sent to higher levels, the project hit the fan. The greatest secrecy was clamped on it, which seemed to indicate military implications in space, and it looked as though we were taking something away from NASA that they didn't have yet. I now have had the two volumes of that project unclassified, and I think that one of these days this is another story that should be told.

But what if after General Trudeau retired from the military in 1962, part of Project Horizon was picked up after all and—either without Soviet involvement or in cooperation with the Soviets because we were facing a common threat from extraterrestrial aliens—we did manage to land a communications tower on the dark side of the moon that turned up on Karl Wolfe's photos? Whether or not we had the technological expertise to pull off such a feat is one question, but the fact that a moon base was in the planning stages prior to 1959 is a documented fact, now available to anyone who wants to read the two volumes of Project Horizon.

A History of Strange Lunar Sightings

For something that's supposedly nothing more than a chunk of dead rock, the moon through recorded history has had a lot of strange activity surrounding it. People have seen lights of different colors, emissions of gaseous substances, and even what's been called volcanic activity. But there are other facts about the moon that, at first glance, seem to defy traditional beliefs about the object.

First of all, the moon is unique. Most people believe that the moon was either formed at the same time as the Earth or spun off from the Earth when the planet was still a molten mass. Other theories put forth that a huge asteroid hit the Earth when it was very young, and the debris and dust that flew off the Earth formed the moon and its nearly perfect orbit. No matter what the theory of the moon's formation, most scientists assume that the Earth and the moon were probably part of one single planet at the dawn of geological history and that they're made of the same substances. But the chemical composition of the moon rocks brought back by the astronauts doesn't really confirm what scientists expected them to.

On the one hand, the composition of the moon rocks seems to indicate that they were much older than the Earth, possibly by a billion years. And the moon dust is a billion years older than the rocks. If this is true, then the moon dust is even older than our solar system. Could this mean that the moon was created somewhere else and not in our solar system? If so, how did it get here? Maybe the moon itself was a huge free-floating planetoid that got trapped in the Earth's orbit. But no other moon in our solar system has a nearly perfect circular orbit like Earth's moon, and no other moon keeps only one side constantly facing the mother planet. Actually, the moon behaves more like the artificial satellites we ourselves launch than like the other moons of our solar system.

Then there's the problem of the NASA seismic readings that were registered when Apollo 12 jettisoned the ascent stage of its booster and it crashed back to the lunar surface. Apollo managers were astonished when the moon reacted more like a hollow bell than a solid planet at the impact and kept reverberating for minutes. "It was like a gong," one NASA scientist was quoted as saying, but then NASA dropped the matter completely and never mentioned it again. Does the moon have an identity that NASA has been trying to keep secret after it coopted the army's plan to place a military base on the lunar surface? Is the moon really a hollow structure and not a solid planetoid after all?

NASA Technical Report R-277

Strange lights, surface eruptions, and floating clouds have been reported for many centuries by lunar observers, some of whom are reputable astronomers. In 1968 NASA published a catalog of over 570 descriptions covering observations from the years 1540 to 1967. Called the NASA Technical Report # R-277 or "Chronological Catalog of Reported Lunar Events," the document lists such things as floating lights above the moon, volcanoes erupting through the lunar surface, lightning flashes, an actual white cloud, and, all the way back in 1587, a star that magically appeared through the points of the crescent moon. Just over a hundred twenty years ago an observer reported a beam of light burning across a crater, and five years after that, shadows that seemed to move across the moon's surface. One of the most active areas of events is inside the crater Plato, where observers have seen lights for hundreds of years. Some of the reports are so bizarre, they seem to defy conventional reality.

For example on March 5, 1587, during the reign of Queen Elizabeth I and while Shakespeare and Christopher Marlowe dominated the English stage, an anonymous observer wrote, "A sterre is sene in the bodie of the moon on the [blank] of Marche, whereat many men merueiled, and not without cause, for it stode directly betwene the pointes of her hornes, the mone being chaunged, not passing 5 or 6 daies before." And in 1714 Cotton Mather reported that nearly fifty years earlier in 1668, several New Englanders saw a "bright starlike point" in a dark area of the moon. On November 12, 1671, a 1720 reference states, observers could see a "small whitish cloud" in the region of Pitatus and a "nebulous appearance" near Mare Crisium three months later on February 3, 1672. On October 18, 1678, there is note of a "white spot," again in the region of Pitatus. On and on for five hundred years, well into the 1950s and 1960s, there are continuing reports, some from highly credible sources, of some form of ongoing activity on the moon. Could this be an alien base dating back three or four hundred years?

These reports of lunar anomalies or strange lights and shadows, officially called "lunar transient phenomena" or LTP, have been so persistent and have aroused so much interest among amateur observers as well as NASA's own scientific community that NASA began an operation in the 1960s called "Operation Moonblink" to photograph and investigate these sightings. NASA commissioned observatories around the world to focus on the moon and take pictures of anything that seemed out of the ordinary. Recordable events were taking place so frequently that within a matter of months there was a short list of incidents, and by 1966 the list had grown to almost thirty phenomena. But, maybe for the same reason that prompted so much urgency in Lieutenant General Arthur Trudeau to get an army unit on the moon, NASA never published the photos shot by observatories working for Moonblink. The results of the investigation are still secret.

Other nations' astronomical communities have been far from silent, however, and have reported thousands of incidents of what look like craft moving across the lunar surface. Photographs and motion pictures have shown objects up to a few miles wide moving over the surface inside the moon's largest craters at speeds over

5,000 miles per hour. And other photos show streaks of light that couldn't be lightning as we understand it, but which may represent some form of communication or optical data transfer, flashing brightly against the darkness of the lunar landscape.

In a fascinating 1977 book by George Leonard called *Somebody Else Is on the Moon,* the author, who said he had seen enough photographs to convince him that the moon was not the lifeless piece of rock it was depicted to be, argued that there was alien life on the moon. Evidence was everywhere, he said, both inside the craters as well as on the outside. And he suggested that both the United States and the Soviet Union knew that the same evidence that they saw on the side of the moon facing the Earth was just as prevalent on the dark side as well. In other words, not only was there evidence of life on the moon—evidence that has been observed for over a thousand years—but the superpowers as far back as the 1950s knew there was life and got into a race to get there first. Could this have been the driving force behind General Trudeau's almost desperate attempt to get the army to the moon before any Soviet forces arrived there? Maybe it was more than just a first strike against an alien presence. Maybe there was a race between the superpowers not just to get to the moon first, but to structure some sort of deal with whatever alien race was already there and use the moon as a base to observe Earth.

At the time General Trudeau was advocating that the army and the president support Project Horizon, he was already firmly in charge of army R&D, a command that before Arthur Trudeau took over was little more than a logistics command. Yet, Trudeau, a technically trained engineer who came out of the Army Corps of Engineers, had already laid his eyes on what would be the Roswell file he would turn over to his deputy, Lieutenant Colonel Philip Corso, just a few years later. Trudeau knew through conversations with many of the German rocket scientists that had been spirited to the United States via Operation Paperclip near the end of the war, that the Germans had also been aware of an alien presence on the moon. Trudeau believed, as did General Douglas MacArthur (who became the head of Sperry-Rand) and President Ronald Reagan (who in the 1980s brought his concerns to the floor of the United Nations General Assembly), that the alien presence on the moon as well as their incursions into our atmosphere represented a threat that we had to counter. And perhaps that inspired his urgency to land an army unit of up to fifteen men on the moon to build fortifications, communications centers, and rocket launching facilities as well. This wasn't just a temporary installation as far as he was concerned. It would be a permanent army base, a tour of duty, an outpost on a new frontier of a very, very bizarre, cold, dangerous war the outcome of which could very well determine the future of humanity on planet Earth.

We Get to the Moon

In one of the classic underground stories about a cover-up of the real truth about the moon, there is a film, obviously suppressed by NASA, of Apollo 11 astronauts planting the American flag into the lunar surface. Then a gust of wind suddenly blows and the flag billows out and flaps in the wind. The astronauts seem to panic for a moment, but then they run toward the camera and cover the lens. What was the source of the gust of wind when there isn't supposed to be any air on the moon? Was the billowing flag just an example of some natural occurrence that had been misinterpreted? NASA never explained it, and in subsequent missions the flags sent with the astronauts had wires inside them to keep them stretched out.

But the billowing flag was not the only strange occurrence that greeted American astronauts on the moon. A photograph taken by Apollo 12's Pete Conrad of his fellow astronaut Alan Bean standing on the moon's surface reveals a strange reflection in Alan Bean's faceplate. We've all seen the wonderful NASA astronaut moon photos in which an American flag is reflected in the faceplate or the image of the astronaut taking the photo. However, reflecting in Alan Bean's faceplate, just above the image of photographer Pete Conrad, is a strange object that looks to be both geometric and artificial hovering over the moon's surface. What's even more strange, when you look at blowups of the photo, is that the hanging object seems to be casting a shadow on the moon's surface. This is important because it means that the object isn't just an illusion formed by the play of light on the camera lens or bouncing off Alan Bean's faceplate. The shadow means that something is really there.

An enhancement of the photo shows that there's more to the object: what analysts have described as a suspension structure holding the object in place. In other computer enhancements, a photo that seems to show Bean carrying his science package turns out to show a large structure in the background behind him. Mars and lunar researcher and writer Richard Hoagland has suggested that the astronaut is standing in front of a large, probably artificial, ancient ruin. Hoagland, who has argued that NASA consistently suppresses information about ruins on the surface of Mars, including a Sphinx-like face, pyramids, and what look to be fortifications, claims that NASA has also suppressed information about ruinlike structures on the surface of the moon.

But one of the most incredible acts of suppression of information, many UFO researchers argue, is the censorship of communication between astronauts and mission controllers about the types of UFO sightings astronauts have experienced on the moon. For example, in one of the most astounding stories, Apollo 11 astronaut Neil Armstrong was said to have reported that extraterrestrial aliens had an established base on the moon and warned the Americans to get off the lunar surface, pronto. According to reports that still remain unconfirmed, both Armstrong and "Buzz" Aldrin saw UFOs on the moon shortly after their landing in July 1969. And in one of the few early uncensored radio transmissions, some viewers even remember hearing one of the astronauts refer to a "light" in a crater. There followed a request from mission control for further information, but the rest of the radio message was never heard on the air. According to a former NASA employee named Otto Binder, ham radio operators monitoring the Apollo radio transmissions with their own VHF receiving facilities picked up the following exchange:

NASA: What's there? Mission Control calling Apollo 11 . . .

APOLLO 11: These "babies" are huge, Sir! Enormous! OH MY GOD! You wouldn't believe it. I'm telling you there are other spacecraft out there, lined up on the far side of the crater edge. They're on the Moon watching us!

In a later interview, Armstrong was reported to have said, "It was incredible, of course we had always known there was a possibility; the fact is, we were warned off. There was never any question then of a space station or a moon city." When asked how the astronauts were "warned off," Armstrong was said to have replied, "I can't go into details, except to say that their ships were far superior to ours both in size and technology. Boy, were they big, and menacing. No, there is no question of a space station."

But there were missions already planned after Apollo 11, and Armstrong reportedly explained that NASA was committed publicly to going to the moon and couldn't suddenly cancel out the later missions. However, the missions were short, the astronauts didn't stay on the moon a moment longer than they had to, and the missions only involved, in Armstrong's words—according to people who heard one of his interviews—"a quick scoop and back again."

Neil Armstrong, according to a Russian scientist who heard the radio transmissions, relayed the message to Mission Control that two large, mysterious objects were watching them after having landed near the moon module. But this message was never heard by the public. And another Russian scientist reported that Buzz Aldrin took color movie film of the UFOs from inside the module, and continued filming them after he and Armstrong went outside. Years later, Neil Armstrong was said to have confirmed that the story was true but that he couldn't talk about it because the CIA wanted the story covered up.

In an issue of *SAGA Magazine* from March 1974 there are other transcripts of conversations between Apollo astronauts, and in some cases the command module pilot and even mission control. In one spectacular exchange during Apollo 15 from August 1971, astronauts David Scott and James Irwin remark about structures they see on the moon's surface that can only be artificial. In describing an array of structures on the lunar landscape, they come upon what they describe as "tracks."

IRWIN: Tracks here as we go down the slope.
CAPCOM: Just follow the tracks, huh?
IRWIN: We know that's a fairly good run. We're bearing 320, hitting 350 on range for 413 . . . I can't get over those lineations, that layering at Mount Hadley.
SCOTT: I can't either. That's really spectacular.
IRWIN: They sure look beautiful.
SCOTT: Talk about organization.
IRWIN: That's the most organized structure I've ever seen.
SCOTT: It's so uniform in width.
IRWIN: Nothing we've seen before this has shown such uniform thickness from the top of the tracks to the bottom.

How could organized, uniformly wide "tracks" wind up on the moon through a natural occurrence? It would seem that they would have to be laid out or laid down somehow by artificial means, possibly as part of a lunar highway system for some other entity occupying the moon. But the Apollo 15 story is even more intriguing because the actual lunar module itself reported that it sighted objects that looked like they were being "propelled" toward them. Was one of our lunar missions attacked by aliens guarding the moon?

CAPCOM: You talked about something mysterious.
ORION (lunar module): O.K. Gordy, when we pitched around, I'd like to tell you about something we saw around the LM. When we were coming about 30 or 40 feet out, there were a lot of objects, white things, flying by. It looked like they were coming out, it looked like they were being propelled or ejected, but I'm not convinced of that.
CAPCOM: We copy that, Charlie.

There might certainly be a natural explanation for this phenomenon, but NASA rarely addresses these types of anomalies straight on, and most of the astronauts are bound by oaths of confidentiality that prohibit them from speaking openly about what, if any, UFO activity they saw on their missions. But throughout NASA files there are descriptions of domelike structures on the moon, triangular structures, and even pyramids or spires. If the moon is indeed a kind of base that's loaded with artificial structures, it's no wonder whoever built them, if the entity is still there, might have wanted us off the moon with the least amount of trouble.

Colonel Philip J. Corso has publicly stated that sources

deep inside military intelligence told him that NASA had to complete the missions it had been committed to sending to the moon because there would be no way to explain to the public why the Apollo program was scrubbed. However, NASA never did build the moon base it had promised the army, and after the final Apollo mission, not one more astronaut has ever set foot on the moon. Corso believed what Armstrong had said about NASA's being warned by aliens to stay off the moon, and it heeded the warning because there was no way it could defend a moon base against more powerful alien weapons.

There are other intriguing discoveries that came out of the Apollo missions and unmanned orbiter missions of the past thirty-five years. Besides the seismic evidence that the moon may be hollow, there is continued trace evidence that the moon may also have contained water at one time and was not the dry piece of rock people have called it. There is also evidence of continued volcanic activity over a period of time or some source of internal warming that continues to radiate heat even when the moon is in eclipse. In his *Alien Agenda,* author Jim Marrs, who also talks about the pioneering research in George Leonard's *Somebody Else Is on the Moon* and of Don Wilson, who wrote *Our Mysterious Spaceship Moon,* documents the still classified research NASA scientists conducted on the composition of the moon that reveals, astonishingly, that Apollo astronauts discovered there was evidence of processed metals on the moon.

A hollow moon? Processed metals? A hard mineral lunar surface containing titanium? Evidence of water in oxidized rocks? Strange vapors that come out of the moon's surface? A nearly circular orbit that almost never occurs in nature and geological processes that were under way on the moon even before they started on the Earth? What does all this point to? It certainly points to a very different picture of the moon from the one most people are given to believe. It points to a planetoid that exhibits some disturbing qualities of an artificial satellite, possibly a colony itself generating heat and energy and housing facilities for who knows what as it circles the Earth.

Lunar Structures

In 1995, Don Ecker—*UFO Magazine* news director and host of the radio talk show *Strange Daze*—described the history of lunar anomalies in an article in the magazine. He described not only the mystery lights but actual structures on the moon that seemed to appear as if they were erected by construction crews within days.

The Bridge

Ecker's article reported that New York *Herald Tribune* science writer John J. O'Neill himself discovered what he described as a "bridge" that looked as though it were straddling a crater. O'Neill reported his sighting of this twelve-mile-long structure to the Association of Lunar and Planetary Observers, who laughed at his observation and told him he was mistaken. Then, one month after O'Neill's report, British astronomer Dr. H. P. Wilkens came forward to report that he, too, had seen the bridge and told the BBC in an interview: "It looks artificial. It's almost incredible that such a thing could have formed in the first instance, or if it was formed, could have lasted during the ages in which the moon has been in existence." The existence of the bridge was confirmed once again by Patrick Moore, another member of the British Astronomical Association, who said that it had appeared too suddenly to have been a natural occurrence. Patrick Moore, Ecker wrote, cataloged an entire list of lunar transient phenomena keyed to specific areas of the moon and to specific craters such as Plato, Poseidonius, and Erastosthenes.

The Shard

Photographed by the pre-Apollo unmanned Lunar Orbiter 3 and described by independent geologist Dr. Bruce Cornet, the shard is an object that stands a mile-and-a-half high from the moon's surface. Its "spindly" shape contains "a regular geometric pattern with constricted nodes and swollen internodes." Geologists agree with Bruce Cornet that it's highly unlikely that such an object can result from natural forces. Dr. Cornet himself said that "No natural process can explain such a structure."

The Tower

Standing close to the shard, the tower is a major five-mile-high structure that's been photographed from five different angles and two different altitudes. Don Ecker's *UFO Magazine* article quotes Dr. Cornet as saying that in all photographs of the tower, "the same structure is visible and can be viewed from two different sides. The Tower exists in front of and to the left of the Shard in the Lunar Orbiter III-84M photograph. The top of the Tower has a very ordered cubic geometry, and appears to be composed of regular cubes joined together to form a very large cube with an estimated width of over one mile."

Like the shard, the tower looks as though it were built by some alien race, almost certainly not by human beings—unless we've been launching secret missions to the moon since the 1950s. The Lunar Orbiter photos exist and are on file at NASA, but you won't find them at the NASA Web site (www.nasa.gov) because NASA won't release them.

The Moon Is Occupied

Author George Leonard wrote in *Somebody Else Is on the Moon* that after examining all of the NASA lunar photographs he could get his hands on it was clear to him that some alien race from outside the solar system had occupied the moon and were using it as a base. He writes, "Evidence of their presence is everywhere, on the surface, on the near side and the hidden side, in the craters, on the maria, and in the highland. They are changing its face. Suspicion or recognition of that triggered the U.S. and the Soviet moon programs."

George Leonard is saying only what appeared to him as obvious, not as wild speculation. And those who report what he said and continue the research, such as Don Ecker and Jim Marrs, have even more data about anomalies on the moon to report on. But it was Lieutenant General Arthur Trudeau who best expressed the urgency underlying the military's thinking. Trudeau served in Korea under General Douglas MacArthur, another army general who said in the 1950s that the next major war the United States would fight would be against enemies in outer space battlefields. What did MacArthur and Trudeau know as truth that the rest of us have yet to be told?

CHAPTER 9

Alien Abductee Stories

"The Air Force has constantly misled the American public about UFOs. I urge Congressional action to reduce the danger from secrecy."

Vice-Admiral Roscoe Hillenkoetter, Director of the Central Intelligence Agency, purported member of MJ-12, and Pacific Commander of Intelligence during World War II, *New York Sunday Times*, February 28, 1960

WITHIN THE UFO RESEARCH COMMUNITY, PERSONAL STORIES of alien abduction can raise some of the most controversial issues. Partly because the stories, when the events are not witnessed by others, are almost completely subjective, and partly because some of the stories relate events that go beyond the fantastic into the spiritual and prophetic, many people who lead routine everyday lives have a hard time suspending credulity to buy into them. But the stories keep coming out and therapists such as Dr. John Mack suggest that there are numerous commonalities to the stories that break across social backgrounds and national borders. Other therapists and researchers such as David Jacobs see a real threat posed by extraterrestrial abductors, who menace their victims with harmful experiments and the inflicting of traumatic experiences. Many of these victims report having been abducted from the time they were small children. In Whitley Streiber's latest book, *Confirmation,* as well as in his first novel about abduction, *Communion,* he describes a similar phenomenon in which there really is no such thing as "adult onset abduction." If you're an abductee, you've been one from the time you were a child, and it's likely your parents were abductees as well.

It's no surprise, therefore, that one of the astounding things Ed Walters says he discovered when he underwent regression therapy after the initial Gulf Breeze sightings years ago was that he'd been abducted when he was a child and had a long series of experiences with the aliens who, he thought at first, had just seemed to turn up out of nowhere to hover over his house in Florida. And Ed Walters's revelations are just one example among thousands in which people retrieve memories that go back all the way to early childhood, some of which they are able to confirm from childhood friends who were witnesses, of bizarre events involving missing time, strange scars and bruises, and bizarre nightmares about figures in gray skintight suits with large insectlike black eyes who lead them by the hand through an other world surrounding.

Alien abduction stories are also very popular in the media. They form the basis not only of motion pictures, but of popular television shows such as *The X-Files* and Steven Spielberg's *Taken* on the Science Fiction channel. Because they're such popular fiction motifs, the real truths behind abduction stories sometimes get lost beneath the fictional elements surrounding whatever reality there is to

he event. But the majority of people who report abduction stories and lay open their lives to absolute derision
and sensationalism have a lot to say about the entities
who they say abducted them. And this is one of the foun-
dations of their experiences that UFO researchers home
in on because it's one of the few anecdotal elements where
extraterrestrial creatures turn up to be analyzed.

Many ufologists say that abductions are real and are
taking place worldwide, involving a large segment of
the human population. There are abductions for the purposes of examination and monitoring, some ufologists
say, and abductions for the purposes of cross-breeding
and hybridization of the species. No matter what the
reason, there are indications, based on the reports of abductees and therapists, that people are being picked up
in the millions and that what happens to them correlates
to the methods we use to study the behavior of our own
wildlife and animals. Watch any nature show, ufologists
say, and you'll see researchers catch, tag, and take fluid
or tissue samples from animals to study their genetics,
social interaction, mating behavior and patterns, and
physical development. Abductees report that encounters
with aliens take place along family lines. The same can
be said for our research on troops of monkeys or ba-
boons or even families of dolphin. However, in the case
of alien abduction, what complicates the parallel between extraterrestrials and our own animal research is
the complexity of ET technology, which is designed for
experiments beyond our own capacity to evaluate.

The alien technology at issue varies from race to race,
ufologists say, with some technology only a couple of
generations in advance of ours and others clearly be-

longing to a whole other paradigmatic category. But even the most bizarre and unnatural experiences people report don't necessarily mean that the technology they're experiencing goes beyond three or so generations. Antigravity envelopes that seem to float people through the air, telekinetic communication or psychic probes, and even the extraction of human cells for in vitro fertilization of another entity are all within our imaginative grasp. Some ufologists point out that human experiments with gene manipulation and the cloning of animals comport almost exactly with what some experiencers report the aliens have done to them. Antigravity experiments go back as far as the 1920s in the United States. And telekinetic communication, especially remote viewing, was the research darling of both the CIA and the KGB as recently as the 1960s and '70s. (Some people report that the research continues to this very day, only this time within the R&D facilities of Fortune 500 corporations.)

The Abduction Experience

If there can be such a thing as a "standard" abduction experience, here is what abductees most commonly report. The aliens seem to come mostly at night. They try to isolate the abductee from everyone else, either by making sure he or she is alone or by rendering anyone nearby incapable of movement. Abductions can occur anywhere, experiencers have reported, not only in the backwoods or out on a lake. People have been abducted from the middle of New York City, out of high-rise apartments or even offices. In other words, if you can

Bubble

Patch

Courtesy Constance Clear.

Other abductees report being floated up into a large "mother ship" inside a bubblelike structure.

see flying triangles floating over the West Side Highway from your own apartment, they can locate you.

A person might awaken from a deep sleep to see a small figure standing in the darkness at the foot of the bed. Maybe the abductee will think it's a dream or a nightmare and try to yell or get up and run. But it's no use, because the abductee has no feeling in any of his or her limbs. Only the eyeballs seem to work. If the abductee can force a scream into the darkness, no one can hear it because all are in a neurological state of suspension. More than one abductee has reported that his or her spouse has slept through the entire incident, even when the spouse's eyes may appear to be wide open.

Then, like the experience Ed Walters reported, the abductee is caught in a colored light, usually blue, and floated out of the house. Closed windows or locked doors? No problem; abductees seem to slip right through solid objects. Some have even reported having been transported right through the roof of the car.

More often than not, according to those who've reported these experiences, the craft they're taken to is not an especially large ship. Some are no more than thirty or so feet across. But they are held in some kind of suspension on this ship until it meets up with or docks with a huge craft abductees call a "mother ship." When one is beamed directly into a mother ship from his or her bed, an abductee can usually report the sensation of floating over rooftops and entire communities where, to their horror, they see the ground from thousands of feet in the air while they ride a beam into the belly of a behemoth craft. Many abductees report that they are returned with scrape marks and abrasions from tree branches they were dragged through on their way to the craft. And some abductees from hospitals have said that when they awoke in their own beds, their gowns or pajamas were on backward, and they had no memory of taking them off. When they asked nurses or attendants, people thought they were crazy.

Once on the mother ship, abductees have said, there can be one or more kinds of alien races. Although the predominant memories are of little gray creatures with large black eyes, all kinds of others are possible. People have described their encounters with tall, Nordic-like beings, reptilian-like creatures, tall and spindly versions of small grays, and even praying mantis types—only six

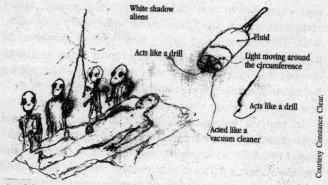

An abductee's rendition of the medical experiments the aliens performed and the type of apparatus they used.

feet tall. The variety of creatures is such that some UFO researchers have speculated that perhaps a war is being waged somewhere in the universe and our planet is one of the distant battlegrounds where one race or another may win a small victory only to lose it again in another skirmish. Perhaps human beings are the hostages in the middle of it all as each side tries to find out what the other learned about the inhabitants of this planet.

Among the various kinds of procedures abductees describe being subjected to on board the mother ship is the collection of bodily fluids, including sperm and ova, and the taking of skin, hair, or fingernail samples. In many instances, living fetuses are extracted by the aliens and taken away while the human parents, some of whom didn't even know they were pregnant, are forced to lie on operating tables until their alien hosts have finished. Some of the aliens have even told their abductees that they're trying to hybridize a species and have shown human beings examples of the children they've parented. Other abductees report being implanted with metallic devices, while still others report having had types of surgeries on their heads and necks. Abductees report being tested in devices that look like CAT scan machines or undergoing holographic experiments in which the aliens gauge their reactions to various types of environmental stimuli.

In perhaps the most bizarre of situations, abductees have said they were paired with other abductees and stimulated sexually while their alien captors watched. If the abductees didn't perform as expected, the scenarios would be enhanced until the abductees demonstrated human mating habits for their audiences. Whether these scenarios were intended to stimulate a natural arousal for the collection of egg and sperm or whether they were meant to fertilize an egg naturally, an egg that would be harvested for genetic manipulation, the abductees were never told. They do talk about their severe posttraumatic reactions to what they say they're put through, psychological reactions that many times require treatment to identify the different "screen memories" that aliens plant to bury the truth from the subjects of their experiments. There are even memories, some of which are recovered as a result of therapy, of adult alien/human hybrids who assist the grays in the experiments and seem to display some empathy for the human abductees, almost as if they're caretakers specifically bred to deal with the humans.

When the abduction is over, the subjects are returned, usually to where they've been taken from, with only a vague, uncomfortable feeling that something happened to them. Most abductees experience what therapist Budd Hopkins and writer Whitley Streiber have called "missing time," an awareness that a chunk of time has dropped out of their lives. It's as if they've been asleep but don't realize it until they look at a clock and discover that three or four hours are simply gone and they can't account for what happened during those hours. In order to recover the memories, many abductees who claim missing time visit abduction therapists, who specialize in dealing with abductees.

Many memories of what happened during missing time are recovered through hypnotic regression, itself so controversial that many states will not allow subjects of hypnotic regression to testify about recovered memories in court. Done improperly, hypnotic regression therapy can actually implant memories, by suggesting a scenario that the subject paints in from his or her own imagination. Nevertheless, regression therapy has become a popular method of recovering missing time memories and has resulted in many stories about abduction experiences, bolstered by the external evidence of bruises, scratches, terminated pregnancies, and strange implants.

In a 1988 comparison of alien abduction stories to dream visions and other psychological states of paranormal perception, *UFO Magazine* editor in chief Vicki Ecker suggests that the commonalities among abduction reports extend far beyond the basic beam up, medical examination and testing, and return to a state of confusion and disorientation. Many subjects report reaching a transcendent state of enlightenment in which they receive either a revelation or the ability to perceive things that will take place in the future. For some abductees, the revelations are so intense, they take the form of prophetic visions, insights that the abductees are expected to share with others. If the abductees are reluctant to share the information they've gained, their confidence is bolstered through subsequent encounters in which they're encouraged to share what they've been taught. This scenario so fits delusional patterns of behavior that even the most steady and rational individual reporting such an experience seems less than credible when telling the story.

Are these events merely psychological? Is there a kind of spiritual basis for these experiences? Or, taken at face value, can these experiences actually be real? Perhaps the best way to judge the credibility of the stories is to evaluate them for themselves. At certain points, the abductees no longer try to convince an incredulous public. Most of them say they have to live within a private hell. They share their stories within support groups of other abductees only, to see how their experiences correlate and to try to make some sense out of the ongoing intrusions into their lives.

Pam Hamilton

In describing her experiences in a 1998 interview for *UFO Magazine,* Pam Hamilton says that the first race of aliens she encountered when she was growing up in a stately Victorian home in Indiana were the grays, little three-and-a-half- to four-foot creatures who visited her while she was in her crib. They would hide in the large closets in her room, she remembers, and at night, after the lights were turned off and her parents had gone to bed, the grays would come out of the closets and reach through the bars of her crib to touch her. She doesn't know how she remembers this, but she can still see the tiny thin hands and arms reaching through the bars of her crib to get her to stand up.

These creatures were small, she remembers, but they had oversized heads, "too big for their bodies," and large black eyes. They were so thin they looked like they were starved, but they weren't menacing or hostile. Pam thought they actually looked like other children and not like strange creatures or something to be afraid of. "They wanted me to play," she says. "But I'm not even old enough to walk yet." She recognizes that these are very early memories, maybe even too early to have been retained naturally, but they are somehow "locked in," as are all her memories of visitations from these and other creatures. "They had big black eyes. They had just a little slit for a mouth and just a little mark for a nose. They had no ears, no genitalia, no clothing on, just their skin."

As she got older, she says she met a new companion, a tall creature with very pale skin and fair hair that, like the grays, communicated with her telepathically. The Nordics—at first a male and then a female—became constant companions, sometimes even materializing when she was with other people. The female still shows up, Pam says, and even after all these years has shown no signs of aging.

In one of the first memories of contact with the Nordics, Pam recalls looking up from the alphabet blocks she was playing with and seeing a strange creature who communicated to her that she had nothing to fear. In subsequent contacts, the creature imparted specific dates

Courtesy Christine "Kesara" Dennett.

Artist Christine "Kesara" Dennett's depiction of a "gray," the alien often described by abductees.

into her mind along with images associated with those dates. For example, she remembers him telling her that "2012 would be very important to me. I would be leading people through the mountains. What mountains? I have no idea. He said as I grew I would know certain things." Yet, in her conversations with other abductees, she's learned that her experiences are not unique. There is a sense among people who've been abducted that they have something inside of them that will "switch on" at some point. Pam says none of this is scary, at least to her, because she's had so many experiences going all the way back into her early childhood.

In her visitation experiences with other aliens, she says that she has seen their craft, actually flown in it, and has been overwhelmed at its size and configuration. "It's a pretty good size," she remembers. "It's big, about the size of a skyscraper if laid down on its side. It's quite big and has a gray metallic look to it. On the controls inside it has symbols. There is a room that they take me into all the time that I call the chart room. It's full of maps. It's like a classroom. There are two other abductees that I know and we were all on the same craft in the same chart room together at the same time. This was about 1993."

She says that she has also seen the controls of the craft and how the aliens operate the ship. "There are panels. You just use your palm, you just press. When I am there in that craft in that environment, I just know. I know how everything works. I know just what to press. It's a different state of consciousness. Whenever they are doing things with me, on these occasions I am more focused than I normally am. I know this sounds very confusing. When I was growing up, somehow I knew instinctively that I didn't belong here. I wasn't like the rest of the kids. I wasn't from here. And when I'm with them, I'm home."

If the Nordics and the grays knew of each other's existence, Pam reports, they didn't seem to acknowledge it. She says that they never turned up together and that she was visited only by grays until she was about three. The small grays still came after the first Nordic showed up, she says, but not as often, and they gradually stopped visiting her until she was much older. Then she saw a different type of gray. This one contacted her when she was outside her house, arriving in a kind of orange-red fireball. "I would see it go across the mountain, and as soon as I saw it, I knew that in a few minutes I was going to see him."

Pam Hamilton's children have also experienced contact and abduction phenomena. For reasons known only to them, the aliens seem to trace patterns they're looking for in their examinations through families. She says that her eldest son even before the age of two had told her about a group of little friends that had appeared to him in his room and wanted to play with him. It reminded her of her first experience with the grays, and she simply told him that she knew all about it. Then her younger daughter began talking about strange little figures who wanted to make friends with her as well, and Pam knew that whatever had communicated with her was now in contact with her children.

The results of alien testing on Pam are evidenced by bruises and scoop marks on her body and limbs. These marks, very apparent when she awakens in the morning, usually disappear within forty-eight hours. Since she's had them most of her life, she decided to start taking photographs of them just to maintain a record of evidence of the kinds of physical marks she's sustained. Her children, now adults, also wake up with marks that tend to go away after a few days and have their own stories about alien contact. Some might argue that the children are merely mimicking what their mother might have told them, but Pam maintains that she held her stories about alien visitations very secret and never disclosed to her children what had happened to her. "All the years my children were growing up, they never knew anything about my experiences. I never told," she explains. "I did not divulge any of this to my children until 1992. They still have not heard all of it. They were never contaminated with any information."

Pam and her children are typical of other abductees in their fears that the government knows about their abductions and shadows them from time to time to gather surveillance on what happens to them. Although many abductees admit there's a certain amount of paranoia in statements like this—"the government follows me to see what the extraterrestrials are learning from us and what information they're giving us"—it's nevertheless disconcerting, Pam says, to see dark vans parked outside her house from time to time and to hear her daughter tell her that she, too, sees dark vans lurking across the street from her house.

"My daughter gets followed," Pam says. "Neighbors have reported seeing large dark sedans and sometimes vans sitting outside her home. They all have dark tinted windows. One of the neighbors, an elderly woman, has called the police on several occasions to report these vehicles. The local police have never been able to track down who the cars belong to. The vans have followed my daughter home from work. They have even followed her to the store." It's for that reason, Pam explains, that her daughter is actually more afraid of those driving the dark cars than she is of any alien visitors.

Courtesy Christine "Kesara" Dennett.

The other alien frequently described by many abductees is the "reptile."

One of Pam's most dramatic discoveries of the military's involvement with extraterrestrials took place in Palmdale, California, in 1992 and 1993 near the Tehachapi Mountains, where the air force maintains an underground base. "The residents who live around·there see a lot of strange stuff," Pam says. "Some things most people would not even believe." She describes what she calls a "Wolfman," a hairy creature right out of the old 1940s movies that she's seen amid members of the military. It was kind of weird, she said, seeing this creature who seemed human in many respects but also resembled one of the "wolfmen" that have glandular problems and turn up from time to time in the evening news or in newspaper feature articles. She said that she even heard him speak to military personnel in a kind of low guttural sound, although he spoke English as if he knew it perfectly. Other people have seen this creature as well, she says, and for those who live near the mountain base, it has become a legend.

The first time she saw this creature was during a time when she had begun "snooping" around the base, as she described her activity, because it was so mysterious. She said she had been crawling through gaps in the fences and trying to get onto the grounds of the base with her camera when she first saw the creature. At first she thought she was completely delusional, but when she described it to others, they claimed that they'd seen it, too, and she wondered whether it was part of some kind of exchange program with the military or whether it was one of the many captured aliens that are rumored to be housed at secret military bases around the country.

In 1993 personnel in uniform confronted her and said that they knew she'd had involvement with alien creatures and that she had implants in her eye and in her ear. "Sometimes we have to adjust these things," she said they told her, and whatever they did inflicted a lot of pain. She said that she felt like a Ping-Pong ball, because after the aliens made contact with her, the military would pick her up and monitor what the aliens did. But it all had to do with information that seemed to be stored in the implants that she said the military needed to access in order to find out what the aliens had been up to. It was very frightening, not because of the aliens themselves, but because of the implication that both the aliens and the military were monitoring a specific group of citizens who simply had no control over their own destinies. Between what the military wanted and what the aliens wanted, the abductees were treated simply as a group of informants who had no ability to exercise any rights whatsoever. And if any of them tried to go public to complain about what was happening to them, the military threatened to make their lives a spectacle of public humiliation. "We'll make you look like a total ass if you talk about this," they threatened her.

Pam remembers an incident that took place near the infamous Area 51 in Nevada when she and her husband, Bill Hamilton, thought they saw a craft lifting off. As they were looking at the craft hovering over their heads, Pam remembers that Bill became very nervous because both of them thought they would be taken aboard. Then the aliens floated Bill Hamilton through an opening in the bottom of the craft, where, Pam says, he was escorted by one of the larger gray aliens, the species that visited her after the Nordics had first made their appearance. Bill remembered that he could see Pam standing on the ground while the ship hovered above the desert, and on either side of her were two smaller gray aliens. That comforted him, Pam said, because he knew that the aliens weren't trying to separate the couple. The entire incident, which took less than a half an hour, was really no more than an exchange of information, Pam remembered, because Bill had encountered aliens from the time that he was a teenager.

It was through her husband that Pam also met Yvonne Smith, an abduction therapist and researcher who facilitates a support group in Southern California. The group became very important to Pam, because for most of her life she had kept her experiences to herself. "I kept these things inside. I didn't want to talk to anyone. In the past I had been ridiculed, told that I was crazy, and I'm not. I was told that I was making things up. So I shut up. You just withdraw."

But after Bill brought her to the Close Encounter Research Organization, Yvonne Smith's investigative support group, she met others who had had similar encounters. "That's what helped me," she explains. "I got to listen to the other people and their experiences. Then I wasn't frightened anymore. I knew I was not alone. I thought, wow, this is happening to all of these people."

A lecturer to other groups on UFO research and abductions, Pam explains that she is not out there trying to convince anyone that her experiences were real. She is sharing information just in case someone in the audience feels all alone in his or her misery or thinks that the abduction experiences are just the delusions of persons suffering from a mental disorder. "This is happening all over the world," she says, "to thousands of us, and we're not crazy. And I don't want to hear this crap about sleep disorders. You don't have a sleep disorder in the middle of the afternoon when you're standing up."

Even though Pam firmly believes that when she's had her daytime experiences she's not asleep, there are sleep disorder therapists as well as psychologists who will say that sleep disorders can take place at any point in the day and that people are capable of lapsing into dream states even when they think they're awake. The dream states, which may also involve forms of hypnogogic paralysis, often occupy only a couple of minutes even though the memories of the images may linger for days or months after the event. These may not be full-blown hallucinations, or even delusions, but recurring dreams in which the sensation of flashing images remains and seems like it has transpired for hours when actually it involves only a couple of minutes. This is one of many types of explanations scientists have used to account for abduction experiences that take place during the day when the subject believes he or she is wide awake. But how can it account for the detailed descriptions and the complex interactions many abductees report? In the cases of those who believe that what they're reporting is true, there have to be deeper explanations for the occurrence.

Clifford Stone

UFO researcher and author of *UFOs Are Real* and *Let the Evidence Speak for Itself* Clifford Stone has been describing his encounters with alien spacecraft both on the Internet and in person for the past few years. Stone, a retired U.S. Army sergeant who served both in Vietnam and in Europe, says that his experiences as a member of a military UFO retrievals unit, which operated in complete anonymity because it was part of the army's Nuclear, Biological, Chemical (NBC) retrieval team, al-

Christine "Kesara" Dennett's depiction of an alien hybrid family.

Courtesy Christine "Kesara" Dennett.

lowed him to witness firsthand the military's involvement with alien cultures. The level of involvement was so extensive and the lives of the members of his unit and witnesses to the UFO encounters were so devastated by the military that Stone said he had to find a way to get the real truth out to the public. But he had to do it without violating any of his confidentiality oaths and without putting himself in legal jeopardy.

His plan, he decided, would be to undertake the most thorough and organized search of information the government has on UFOs under the Freedom of Information Act. Once the information was out in public, it's no longer considered confidential information, and Stone could talk about it without violating any of his oaths. This seemed a straightforward plan at first, but Stone was, nevertheless, an enlisted man in the army, and his queries soon came to the attention of a number of his officers, some of whom wanted them stopped.

At first the pressure on Stone to stop looking for UFO documents came in the form of suggestions from officers. There were lieutenants and captains who cautioned him that he was causing trouble, raising people's hackles, and making waves for the officers over him. Wouldn't he want the people whom he served under to be kindly disposed to him, to think he was a team player instead of a troublemaker? Stone said that he was as deferential as he could be to the officers who told him to stop his FOIA research, but that he was still an American citizen with the same rights to file FOIA searches as any other citizen. So the smiles and polite suggestions stopped—and the cautionary suggestions turned into threats. He was flatly told that he was making real enemies in the services and that senior brass in sensitive posts were looking most unkindly on the junior officers to whom Sergeant Stone reported. People were going to go after him if he didn't stop. But Stone didn't stop. In fact, he began finding some real nuggets of information, because having served in the NBC units and on retrievals teams, he knew where to look. Finally, he was given a firm order: stop the FOIA searches or face a court-martial for disobeying orders.

"It wasn't a lawful order," Stone told the superiors who ordered him to give up on his searches. "If it's not a lawful order, I don't have to obey it." And he said that if they ordered him to stand trial, he would do so, but that he couldn't be ordered to cease and desist from an activity that any American citizen is granted to engage in by law, the freedom to pursue public information. The army relented and then tried to discharge him on a medical Section 8, psychiatric. But he resisted that as well and said that all he was doing was looking for documents. Nothing crazy about that even if had to do with UFOs and abductions. Finally the army relented altogether and sent him to Roswell, New Mexico, where he became the military adviser to the cadets at the New Mexico Military Institute, from which posting he retired to begin his research full-time.

What drove Cliff Stone to search out the truth about the government's involvement with UFOs was his own experience as a contactee from the time he was a child. He has told interviewers that he first saw a UFO and its inhabitants in 1957 when he was only seven years old, living with his parents in southern Ohio. Stone remembers that after his first encounters, in which he was taken aboard a craft and met with beings he calls "entities," a military officer began paying visits to his house to make his acquaintance. Stone didn't know it then, but believes now that the military was in contact with alien entities and monitored their contacts with human beings.

Even as far back as the 1950s, Stone says, the military was tracking UFO appearances and investigating reported encounters between human beings and aliens. At first, it was only an intelligence-gathering operation. When there were rumors that a craft had landed and private citizens had seen something emerge, the air force converged on the spot to get as many interviews as possible. When they identified someone who'd been contacted or taken aboard, sometimes they got to know him, maybe even checked back in from time to time, and even tried to get the person into the military. This was a person who knew something few other people did—very few—that there was another form of life that was not human, but more technologically advanced. This person knew there was life on other planets besides Earth. And Cliff Stone was one of these people. He had made contact.

Stone says he was recruited by the army while he was still a teenager in Ohio. By the late 1960s, as the war in Vietnam was heating up, he was indoctrinated into what he believed was the military UFO unit. But it was a backdoor indoctrination, an event set up to show him some of the information that the army seemed to have accumulated on UFOs without anyone ever directly telling him this is what the government knows and what it's doing about dealing with UFOs. It was a spellbinding afternoon, Stone remembers, because it was almost as if it took place by accident, and then he found himself dealing with a UFO retrievals unit that seemed to fall in whenever a UFO crash or shoot-down took place.

His indoctrination began when he was sent to Fort Belvoir on a very routine courier assignment. But when he arrived there, he remembers he was sent to a large room that was almost like a movie theater. The room was dark. Projected onto the screen in front of him was what he thought was a training film. Maybe the projectionist had fallen asleep, he thought. Maybe no one knew there was a training film being shown and it was simply playing to a nonexistent audience. Typical military.

But when he looked at the screen to see what the movie was all about, he thought it was a 1950s science-fiction film. There was what looked like a crashed spaceship. There were military units gathered around it. There were crews hauling debris onto trucks and carting them away. Then the scene changed and it was another spacecraft, a flying crescent as seen through a warplane's gun camera. Then there was another scene on the ground. What was this?

Cliff quickly realized that this wasn't a science-fiction movie, it was a real series of events. No actors here. He was looking at what could only be actual military footage of some kind of strange craft. But it was a craft of a type he'd seen before. Resonating deep in his memory were sensations of having been there, having been *in* exactly the same type of spacecraft he was seeing on the movie screen—and of having encountered the beings who piloted that craft. Viewing the flickering images on the screen felt almost like a dream. But it was no dream. He was in Fort Belvoir looking at something he either was not supposed to see or that was meant specifically for him. What Stone didn't know at the time was that he was actually being indoctrinated into one of the army's most secret units. It is camouflaged under a variety of code names and operations, but it deals with the investigation and retrievals of downed UFOs.

Project Moon Dust and Operation Blue Fly

Sometimes they went in wearing hazardous materials suits to protect them from deadly chemicals spills. At other times they trained as a frontline unit in simulated nuclear disasters. And if biological weapons were used on a distant battlefield, these would be the troops who would go in first to clean up the restricted area. The unit was called "NBC" for nuclear, biological, chemical, and it was where Sergeant Clifford Stone was assigned as a company clerk. But the unit had another, far more secret mission, Stone reveals, that was even more critical to the army than the cleanup after a nerve gas attack or securing an area contaminated by a deadly biological agent. This was the unit, under the cover of a potential nuclear, biological, or chemical disaster, that retrieved downed space debris from foreign space vehicles and, more important, debris of unknown origin. He belonged to a unit, Stone says in his books, *UFOs Are Real* and *Let the Evidence Speak for Itself,* that retrieved downed UFOs from anywhere in the world.

The military's retrieval and return programs were designated formally as "Project Moon Dust" and "Operation Blue Fly" and had been in operation by the air force as early as 1961, according to an air force memo Stone found during a Freedom of Information search. Moon Dust was referred to as a program to "locate, recover, and deliver descended foreign space vehicles." The same air force memo also defines Operation Blue Fly as having been "established to facilitate expeditious delivery to FTD of Moon Dust or other items of great technological intelligence interest." (The "FTD" in this memo is an abbreviation for the Foreign Technology Division, the office inside the Pentagon where Army Lieutenant Colonel Philip Corso served during the years he described managing the "Roswell File" in his book *The Day after Roswell*.) Cliff Stone also found a 1973 State Department memo requiring all its embassies to use the code word "Moon Dust" in those cases "involving the examination of non-U.S. space objects or objects of unknown origin."

Cliff Stone was a part of the military UFO retrieval operations during his tour of duty in Vietnam and afterward in Europe. He has described missions in which both North Vietnamese and U.S. Army units were prevented from recovering their wounded from fire zones by the presence of UFOs over the battlefield. And he's described how army and air force retrievals teams were deployed to secure the areas while the field commanders waited for orders from their superiors. But no mission was as dramatic or frightening as the one that began one night outside the perimeter of his logistics command headquarters in March or April of 1970 with the appearance of some strange colored lights blinking in the air over the neighboring Michelin rubber plantation.

He remembers specifically that the lights couldn't possibly be flares; flares are deployed to light an area beneath them, but these lights did not cast any light. The next night the lights returned, and Stone decided to investigate on his own, grabbing his M-16 and crawling outside the perimeter gate and through the no-man's-land or "kill zone" that surrounded the logistics command base camp. At the edge of the kill zone, along a road that ran parallel to the rubber plantation, Stone met up with a figure he'd seen before: an officer, he thought, who had been in charge of other types of retrieval operations. He told Stone, as if he expected him to be there, that he'd better get a move on if they were going to complete their mission tonight.

Without questioning the officer's commands, Cliff followed him to where a small group of soldiers had been assembled aboard three double-rotor Chinook helicopters. These were not typical troop carriers or gunships but were equipped with electronic surveillance apparatus. The helos whisked the American soldiers to what the leader of the mission called a Viet Cong tunnel complex. Hoping they wouldn't be fired upon by enemy troops as soon as they landed, Stone and the others quickly jumped off the Chinooks and marched up a trail in the Black Virgin Mountains until they reached the mouth of one of the many tunnel complexes that ran through South Vietnam and kept the VC supplied with troops, ammunition, food, and personnel throughout the war.

Most of the tunnel complexes had so many exits that blowing up and sealing off one simply meant that the VC would slip out the others. But this complex was different. When the G.I.'s pulled the camouflage shrubbery away from the entrance, Stone was astonished to see that it was big enough for an eighteen-wheeler to have made its way through. This wasn't just a crawl space, it was an actual highway built into the earth. And unlike the typical VC cave carved out of the rock by hammers and blades, this seemed smooth, as if the rock had been melted, to form shiny walls. And the walls inside the cave were towering. It certainly didn't look as though the VC had worked this cavern with pneumatic tools or dug it out by hand.

The troops made their way down the main entrance, laying down phone cable to stay in contact from the mouth of the tunnel. But as they moved deeper inside, their flashlights and electronic equipment began to malfunction, and at a certain point their radios and lights completely failed. But, oddly enough, even though it was nighttime, the cave gave off a kind of luminescence that enabled the men to see. And as the main party moved deeper into the tunnel, it became lighter and lighter. This shouldn't be. They were deep inside a cave that had no natural light source, and the men's handheld lights had failed. And the mysteries were getting even more disturbing.

Stone asked the mission leader how long this place had been sitting here and why they were the first to reconnoiter it. To his surprise, the older man replied that they'd just discovered the cave a couple of days earlier, at about the same time the lights had made their appearance overhead. Earlier reconnaissance of the area by army units looking for VC tunnels had turned up nothing. How could the VC have constructed an underground complex like this in only a couple of days and kept their activity so well hidden? It didn't make sense. But when they reached the large center room, almost an atrium, it was obvious that neither the Viet Cong nor the North Vietnamese could have dug this place out. It was too deep underground, too large. And the walls had become almost like glass.

As they spread out into the large room, Stone remembers, they began to experience the effects of a heavy electrical field. It engulfed them, slowing them down, making their skin tingle and the hair on their necks and heads crackle and stand up. Cliff Stone knew what static electricity felt like, and he felt as though he were walking through it as he moved toward the far edge of the room and closer to what they all thought was a source of light. The closer they got, the more they could make out details within the light.

It was like nothing they had ever seen before, a strange flat object, three or so feet wide and glowing green. On its surface Stone could make out a series of dials and buttons. If he didn't know any better he would have called it a control panel of some sort, but a panel to control what? They were in the middle of a cave well below the earth's surface.

The mission commander suggested that Stone touch the panel, maybe try to run his hand over some of the controls. Stone was reluctant at first, telling the mission commander that he was as scared as any human being could be. He didn't want to go near the glowing object, much less touch it. Yet he had to admit it was as inviting as it was fascinating. What would happen if he played with a few of the controls? Maybe the mission commander was right, and Stone should see how the thing worked.

Part of what was driving him, he says, was that it all looked strangely familiar. It wasn't as if he had seen the flat panel before, but somehow he knew from old, old memories that it wouldn't hurt him. He also knew that the mission commander knew that Stone was supposed to have some experience with this. Something from very far back in his past was telling him that this was okay.

So he put his hand over one of the indentations and tried to depress part of the controls. And that's when the lights came up.

Suddenly Cliff Stone and the rest of the detail knew they weren't in a natural cave at all, but inside a huge cube. Luminescence emanated from the black shiny walls. On one side of the room was what Cliff Stone described as a cigar-shaped ship with windows along both sides behind which was a deep blue light. All around the room men could now see biological apparatus and human organs floating in large transparent vessels. He could see rows of test tubes and other containers. If Stone didn't know otherwise, he could have believed himself to be in Dr. Frankenstein's laboratory. He could make out the remains of American military personnel, Vietnamese—and some bodies that to him were clearly not human.

And he would have been frightened beyond his wits had the alien bodies he was seeing not been familiar. He had seen them before, these large-headed gray creatures with spindly bodies and arms. There were other alien creatures as well. And he realized that he must be standing inside some kind of medical station or, worse, a morgue where bodies were dissected and stored.

One of the glass test tubes dropped from his hand as he tried to inspect it, but it didn't break as it hit the floor. In fact, this clear substance seemed so strong, it was like nothing he had seen before. He ran his hands over the different vessels containing biological remains.

Then something caught his attention from overhead. Movement. And when he pointed to the ceiling above the ship, they could see their own men, a small detail they'd left outside to establish a perimeter around the cave entrance and maintain communications with the choppers that were their lifeline out of there. The night sky was clear; they could see sentries move back and forth across the area. From Stone's position inside the cave, the men seemed to be walking on air above his head.

The mission leader sent a runner back through the cave with instructions for the patrol detail outside to move around in a prearranged series of maneuvers so that those inside could be sure they were watching their own men. Obviously, the troops outside had no idea that they could be seen from below or that what looked to them like regular grass and dirt was transparent to those in the cave. And for just a minute, a few of the men inside the room laughed at the idea.

Cliff's detail got the order to break down the room and carry every piece of equipment they could lift topside for the choppers to transport. While the men were organized into small details, Stone and the officer in charge tried to figure out how to get the control panel loose so they could take it as well. The thing seemed to be connected to the very walls, and although it wasn't heavy, it was somehow wired into the circuitry of the environmental lighting and air system. Frustrated that they couldn't find any type of detachable plug, since the panel was obviously a component of some sort, Stone just lifted it up and yanked it away from the wall.

A sound exploded in his head and the lights and clear view of the surface went out. Then a series of red, pencil-thin lights started firing across the room, burning and sizzling in the increasingly foul air. Then, even before he knew what was happening, one of the red beams of light hit him in the eye and he staggered under the searing pain. He dropped the control panel, grabbed his eye, and dropped to the floor in agony. Then another searing pain ran up his back. He remembers rolling over and calling out for help. He remembers the sensation of large hands taking hold of him and lifting. And that's all he remembers.

Stone came to at the entrance to the cave, but he was wounded now. One of the waiting Chinooks took him back to base, where he was stretcher-carried into the infirmary. A doctor put a patch over his eye and gave him something for the pain, which by now had begun to subside. His eye would heal, the doctor told him: it was only a burn or an insect bite that was causing an inflammation, but he needed to return the next day for another check. He was okay to walk, but he was on restricted duty until the infirmary docs cleared him.

Outside the base hospital the mission commander was waiting. He took Stone over to a neighboring Quonset hut.

"What exactly do you remember in that cave?" he asked. "Do you remember any alien presence?" Stone says that he was taken aback at first by what the mission commander asked. Then he asked, "Do you remember what happened after you took a hit from that light?"

All Stone could remember was the pain in his eye, a burning pain that felt like a hot needle rotating inside his eyeball. Then there was the pain in his back as if he'd just been hit with napalm. But there was nothing else. He passed out from the pain just as he felt himself being lifted and didn't remember anything until they got him into the helo. So he thanked the mission commander for lugging him outside the cave and was about to say that he should have been more careful about the beams of light, when the man, who wore the uniform of an army colonel, cut him off.

"We were all down, Sergeant," he said, describing how the men in the cave detail were paralyzed before they blacked out. But the mission commander could still see Stone on his feet before he lost consciousness. "All of us, but you," he continued. "You didn't pass out. Something else happened. We were down but for forty-five minutes you were away from us, and we don't know where you went. Something took you away, and I've got to know what that was for sure."

Stone didn't bother to argue. He had no conscious memories of anything but the pain. So when the colonel asked him to take a shot of what they used to call flak juice to recover the memories of what happened to him in the cave, he agreed. If it could help him make sense of the mission, why not? The colonel added that whatever memories he recovered would have to remain completely confidential, not to be shared with anyone.

In Cliff Stone's own words, recorded during an interview over twenty-five years later, he recalled, "After getting hit in the eye with the light and the burning and going down, I didn't pass out. I was in a lot of pain, I was in tremendous pain. Then, a lot of—well, fine, I now have a fascination with grasshoppers, and I guess this is the incident that causes that—these creatures of humanoid shape started to appear. I can remember looking into their faces. These were like big grasshoppers, and I can remember going ahead, and picking up my

M-16, and at that time I was going to shoot. One of them went ahead and grabbed my M-16, but I wouldn't let go and then I heard a voice that I've heard many times before, even through my childhood. I never wanted to bring this up, but it's got to be brought up now. One of the entities that I've always known told me that they had to take care of my eye or I would lose it, that I'd lose my sight. But it would still be sore for a couple of days, and that my people could go ahead and treat it with medications that they had available to them. Once again I was asked, as I was asked several times before by these creatures, 'Why are you here, and what are you doing here? This isn't your nature. You should not be involved in this war.'"

The colonel told Stone that they had come up with a cover story for the entire incident, that the detail had uncovered a North Vietnamese Army storage facility built into a hillside and came under enemy fire. They destroyed what they could and were evacuated out with casualties. One of those casualties was Sergeant Stone, who had gotten stung in his eye by an insect and was taken back with the wounded. The entire incident would go away. But for Cliff Stone, it became one of the driving incidents that forced him to track down the truth about the military's relationships with alien entities and the knowledge the military seemed to have in advance of UFO activity.

In subsequent encounters with alien creatures after his retirement from the United States Army, Stone says, he began to understand more about who the aliens were, why the different races are in conflict with one another, and why the military seemed to know whom to expose to the UFO retrievals training film, as Stone was indoctrinated. Since his release from the army and as his own encounters have continued, Cliff Stone has continued his research into government records. He has been able to predict UFO landings and military encounters with alien craft. Often he has told friends about a sighting that will occur at a specific time and specific place long before the sighting actually occurs. The remote viewing events, he explains, are part of what the aliens provide him, the ability to see forward in time just as if he were traveling. It was why the army recruited him and others like him, he understands now: because they knew that children who had been visited were able to communicate with the entities and exploit the ability to travel in time.

The government has been in contact with alien visitors since before Roswell, Stone tells his audience at his numerous speaking engagements and appearances at the Roswell UFO Museum. Alien spacecraft were spectators during World War II and have been shadowing the aircraft of the world's superpowers ever since. Stone explains that the government has captured aliens, interrogated them, and conducted abductions of private citizens who have had contact with aliens. Because there are so many different alien races visiting our planet and interacting with human beings, the government has had to establish a covert monitoring program of its own citizens in order to keep track of the alien presence on our own planet.

It's this level of activity that Cliff has spoken about at UFO conferences and as a constant radio talk show guest both in the United States and in foreign countries.

It is a message that seems beyond strange but which hits a resonant chord among people who've had their own UFO contact experiences.

The Abductee Movement

There is no question but that the stories of UFO abductions, medical experiments, genetic testing and embryonic implanting, the transfer of information to preferred human contactees, and military abductions as intelligence operations make for some truly unbelievable narratives. Contactees and abductees talk about grays, Nordics, reptilians, and, in Cliff Stone's case, insectlike humanoids. How can we believe all of this?

Both Dr. Jonathan Mack and Professor David Jacobs, author of *The Threat*, caution us that the evidence that something paranormal is going on is overwhelming. Even if some people are making up stories or hoaxing the media, others have everything to lose and nothing to gain. In other words, there are just too many people reporting bizarre yet similar encounters for the alien abduction scenario to be either a mass delusion or a widespread, deliberate falsification.

Some psychologists have said that the entire recovered memory therapy movement is tainted by poor procedure. Recovered memories are themselves constructs, reassemblies of memory fragments that might make no sense until a therapist helps a patient put them into a story context. If that story context is alien abduction, then so be it. If the story context is childhood incest or sexual abuse, then the patient becomes a sex abuse victim in therapy.

In fact, many psychologists claim that inasmuch as the alien abduction stories deal with such basic psychological issues as loss of control, torture and humiliation, physical, emotional, and sexual abuse, invasiveness, and a form of degradation, one could almost describe alien abduction memories as a reaction to sexual torture with alien faces and spaceships as part of a "screening memory" to protect the victim from seeing the actual faces of the perpetrators—who could be her or his own family.

Moreover, many psychologists say, the use of hypnotic regression on the part of an abduction therapist predisposed to the alien abduction theory simply implants the therapist's issues into the patient's mind. This is why many psychologists refuse to deal with alien abduction cases. But, if Mack and Jacobs are correct that alien abduction cases do follow a specific scenario and belong in their own category, then the hundreds of thousands, and possibly millions, of abduction cases are recollections of real events.

If the members of the abductee community find it easy to believe abduction stories told by others because the stories comport with their own experiences, does that lend some credibility to the phenomenon? It could be that the very nature of an alien abduction community, a group of millions of people who report that they've been subjected to visitations by members of alien species, imprisonment on board spaceships or inside medical laboratories, forms of invasive experimentation and telepathic interrogation, and made to supply sexual fluids for medical procedures, means that we're dealing with an ongoing series of events. These are events that the government not only refuses to disclose, but actively aids and abets through its own intelligence procedures or, even worse, an out-and-out deal with the aliens who are perpetrating the abductions. This is, in effect, part of the lawsuit that CAUS's Peter Gersten has filed against the United States government: a demand for a full disclosure in the face of what many people say is overwhelming evidence that there is some truth to the stories of alien abductions. And although some judges may laugh and summarily dismiss these cases because the government claims they violate national security by forcing agencies to reveal intelligence-gathering procedures, the pressure for disclosure is slowly building.

Something truly is going on out there. Too many people have seen or experienced bizarre happenings with strange-looking beings for this to be a calculated hoax or a mass hallucination. Gersten's fundamental argument is simple: The government has guaranteed the individual citizen a basic covenant that it will preserve and protect the rights of the individual citizen as those rights are defined under the Constitution. The government has to protect its citizens from perpetrators of crime and enforce the law against anyone, military or the inhabitants of flying saucers, who threatens the safety and violates the privacy of individual citizens. For that reason alone, whatever the truth behind the alien abduction stories, this is one area where one hopes the truth will ultimately be out there.

CHAPTER 10

The French X-Files

"There should be a serious investigation of authentic reports, and all factual evidence and possible conclusions should be given to the public."

Lieutenant General P. A. del Valle, USMC

REPORTS ON UFOS PROLIFERATE. EVERY SIX MONTHS OR so, one or another group, usually with what they describe as inside information, releases new revelations amid a flurry of testimonials to their legitimacy. The result is a little bubble of excitement, a matching bubble of dispute and argument, and then the disappearance of both. Once in a while, however, a report appears that really does carry legitimacy. Whether based on information that is independently verifiable or because of the political power or academic credibility of its authors, such a report demands more than passing attention. That's what happened in 1998 when the Rockefeller Panel made public the proceedings of its conference at Pocantico and San Francisco (available in book form as *The UFO Enigma: A New Report on the Physical Evidence*, Peter A. Sturrock [New York: Warner Books,

1999]), and again in 1999 when the French COMETA report on UFOs, a formerly confidential report to the prime minister and president of France, was made public.

The COMETA document goes well beyond previous studies citing famous cases of UFO encounters. This astonishing report contains information from deep inside government files. Created by the French Institut des Hautes Etudes de Défense Nationale, or Institute of Higher Studies for National Defense, it is a detailed study not only about encounters with *les objets volant non identifié* (OVNI, the French term for unidentified flying objects), but, more importantly, about the implications of UFOs to French national defense.

The comprehensive three-part study, published in French in a special edition of the magazine *VSD*, moves from some of the most important and compelling cases of UFOs over France and around the world to a summary of methods of investigation and the current state of knowledge. In the final section, the report discusses the implications for national defense posed by the existence of UFOs and their encounters with humans, and recommends cooperation among government agencies. Tellingly, however, the report also suggests an emergency preparedness plan for governments and agencies in the event of an overt contact by extraterrestrials or an outright "Mars Attacks" military invasion.

The report was written by an independent group of researchers and authors called COMETA, or Committee for In-Depth Studies, who worked with the Institute of Higher Studies for National Defense and who specialize in concentrated analysis of comprehensive technology and defense-related issues. Divided into three parts, the report begins with factual and eyewitness testimonies from witnesses to UFO encounters, assesses the current state of knowledge of UFO phenomena, and evaluates issues of national defense in terms of the potential capabilities of UFOs, especially if those UFOs are extraterrestrial in origin. In the final section of recommendations, the authors propose strategies to pursue organized studies into UFO phenomena and ways to amalgamate research into organizations that supersede traditional disciplines and national interests so as to prepare for eventual contact with intelligent beings who, with a quasi-certainty, are extraterrestrial. Coming as it does from highly placed French government, military, and academic figures, this report intimates that an astounding new reality is about to come upon us.

In an introductory statement to the report, General Bernard Norlain, the former director of the Institute of Higher Studies for National Defense, describes how General Denis Letty of the French Air Force came to him back in 1995 with a proposal for a new committee to study the phenomena of UFOs and sought his support for the research project. It was not the first time such a study came to his attention, General Norlain writes; twenty years earlier, a similar plan led to the organization of GEPAN, the first UFO study committee. This new study contained a promise to bring a diverse range of disciplines to bear on a complicated problem. Thus the study supported some of the same issues as the Rockefeller Panel in the United States.

Facts and Testimony

The first section of the report contains compelling stories of pilot encounters with UFOs.

The first incident in the report, the testimony of Mirage IV fighter pilot Henri Giraud and his navigator, takes place on March 7, 1977, late at night in the skies over Dijon as the Mirage is returning from a nighttime training mission. At approximately ninety degrees off their right wing the pilots notice a brilliant light flying at a great speed toward them at the same altitude and on a collision course. They raise the military radar controller on radio, who confirms he has the Mirage on his radar screen but no other contacts. As the pilot and navigator watch the bright light cross their path from approximately three o'clock to eleven o'clock off their left wing, it disappears. As they resume their course back to base, an identical light appears off their right wing on a collision course. The light continues around the plane when it, too, disappears, just like the first one. Again the radar controller can pick up nothing on his screen.

What were these mysterious lights, the report asks, which are attested to by a trained combat flight crew in an advanced fighter? These were not untrained observers on the ground looking into lights that could have been anything floating above them in the sky, these were interceptor pilots flying over home territory, where they would be expected in time of war to identify and home in on hostile aircraft. Therefore, their sighting has to be deemed credible, and all the more amazing inasmuch as their flight controller reported no other contacts on his radar screen.

The next incident in the report is the testimony of Colonel Claude Bosc, the pilot of a T33 jet on a night-time flight with two other aircraft in a loose formation en route from Nantes to Poitiers. Cruising at about 460 km/h, the pilot saw something that looked like a green signal flare that rose as if it had been shot from a gun. However, what he had first thought was a flare stabilized at a level altitude and seemed to turn and fly right at him on a collision course. As the green light, which was less than two meters across, approached his cockpit as if it were a cannon ball, Claude Bosc reflexively crossed his arms across his face in a defensive posture to brace for impact.

But it was an impact that never came. Instead, the aircraft was enveloped in a green phosphorescent light that passed right through the plane and exited after only a couple of seconds. The pilot noticed that the light had something like a comet trail behind it that was the same fluorescent green color as the ball. The entire encounter took only five seconds, the pilot reported, and it was not picked up on radar. However, the other pilots who were following him at one- to two-minute intervals along the same route reported that they, too, saw the entire encounter with the green sphere.

The last of the French pilots' testimonies is Captain Jean-Charles Duboc's narrative of his strange encounter with a bell-shaped UFO. He was in command of Air France flight 3532 out of Nice shortly after noon in gloriously clear weather on January 28, 1994. It was the chief steward, present at that moment in the cockpit, who first noticed the strange object at a sharp angle off to the left of the plane's nose, and pointed out what he thought was a weather balloon to the co-pilot. Captain Duboc wasn't so sure and turned the plane approximately forty-five degrees to get a better angle. That was when all three crew members got a good look at the object and suddenly realized that this was nothing they'd ever seen before, confirming it verbally to one another just to make sure they were all looking at the same object.

The clear skies with high, light clouds afforded the crew members in the Air France cockpit an excellent opportunity to view the object, which was probably less than 1,500 meters below them and 50 kilometers away. They agreed that this was a huge bell-shaped object that suddenly seemed to change shades of color right before their eyes, then disappear as if it suddenly became invisible. Captain Duboc made a report of the sighting to the civil air flight controllers at Reims, who reported having no information that could account for the object they'd reported. According to procedure, the civil controllers forwarded the report to the military air defense operations center and ordered that the pilot file a "near-collision" report immediately upon landing.

Later on it was revealed that the French air defense operations center had recorded a mysterious radar track that stayed on its screen for about fifty seconds at the same time the pilot reported his near collision with the bell-shaped object. The track actually crossed Air France 3532's flight path and could not be correlated with any other aircraft that had filed a flight plan for that day. After crossing the Air France flight path, the object disappeared from all military radars. A subsequent investigation excluded the possibility that the object was a weather balloon.

Aeronautical Encounters in Other Countries

Of all the encounters at aerial bases around the world, perhaps the most famous occurred at Lakenheath-Bentwaters, a joint USAF/RAF airbase thirty kilometers north of Cambridge in the United Kingdom, the site of the 1980 Bentwaters incident (see Chapter 5). The COMETA report examines the nights of August 13 and 14 in 1956, when unknown objects turned up on the base radar screens.

The 1956 incident began at 10:55 P.M. when base radars picked up contacts traveling between 2,000 and 3,000 miles per hour right over the base. Controllers in the Bentwaters tower reported seeing brilliant lights streaking by overhead, as did a pilot in a transport flying over the base. The transport pilot said the lights shot right by him at an incredible speed. Both the tower flight controllers and the transport pilot had visually confirmed the objects that the radar operators had picked up on their screens.

The radar controllers at Bentwaters notified the watch commander of the radar traffic control center at Lakenheath. The search for the objects began. Then the radars picked up an object that seemed to be stationary in the sky about forty kilometers southwest of the base. The watch commander at Lakenheath confirmed the sighting. Suddenly the object moved from a dead stop to a speed of approximately 900 kilometers an hour and crisscrossed the Lakenheath airspace, moving in one direction then another and stopping every few minutes to hang stationary in the air before resuming its supersonic speed.

What was so astonishing was that there seemed to be no period of acceleration. The object had the ability to go from a standstill or stationary hover to supersonic speed in an instant. No known object at that time was capable of that kind of movement. In a Telex sent by Lakenheath, the sender concluded, "The fact that the rapid accelerations and the immediate stops of the object had been detected by radar as well as by visual sighting, as clearly as a sunburst, gave the report absolute credibility. One cannot believe that these observations could be either meteorological or astrological in origin."

Thirty to forty-five minutes after the bizarre radar contacts, the RAF scrambled a two-seater Venom night-fighter to pursue the object. They vectored it toward the strange light now flying ten kilometers east of the control center, at which point the pilot acquired the target visually as well as on radar. Then he lost it. He was vectored to a new position sixteen kilometers east of Lakenheath where he acquired a new target and reported, "My machine guns are locked on it!" But a short time after his transmission, he lost the target again. However, this time the target was tracked by the radar operators at the flight control center, who informed the pilot that the object made a sudden course change and was now on his tail, following him at a short distance.

The pilot of the Venom confirmed the new position and, observed by the radar operators, undertook a series of aerial dogfight maneuvers—climbing barrel rolls, nosedives, and spiraling turns—for the next ten minutes to put himself behind the object. But he didn't succeed, and the UFO kept following him at a constant distance, according to the operators tracking the images on the ground radars. Finally, low on fuel, the pilot returned to base while he radioed his controllers to ask whether the UFO was still maintaining its pursuit of his aircraft. In fact, the UFO had followed him at a short distance and then hovered motionless until it changed direction again, taking off toward the north at 950 kilometers per hour until it disappeared from radar at around 3:30 in the morning. A second Venom interceptor scrambled to replace the first, but returned very quickly because of mechanical problems after having failed to establish any contact with the UFO.

This incident, according to the radar expert on the Condon commission, ranks as one of the most troubling UFO incidents to date because of the high credibility of the observers and the coherence of the entire story. There were simply too many witnesses of high professional caliber, all of them trained for just such an intrusion into their airspace, to have made the kinds of mistakes that would have resulted in a misidentification of the object. It was clearly an event with a high degree of strangeness, according to the COMETA report.

The next reference to a foreign aerial UFO sighting documented in the COMETA report is the July 1957 RB-47 incident over the southern United States (also classified as "unidentifiable" in the Condon Report on UFOs). In this incident, what was apparently a UFO turned up as a signal on military radar as well as a microwave signal and a visual sighting made by officers on the RB-47. The incident was so credible at the time that the military regarded it as vital defense information. In an incredible series of maneuvers, the unidentified object seemed to play hide-and-seek with the aircraft, which tried to remain in visual contact with the object for as long as possible. At the same time, the event was tracked by radars in Louisiana, Texas, Utah, and Oklahoma as it played out in the skies across the southern United States.

Although *Aviation Week* writer Phil Klass later suggested that the incident resulted from completely natural causes, UFO researcher Brad Sparks, as recently as 1997, refuted Klass by saying that the incident was correctly categorized as an unknown object by the Condon Report. The importance of the RB-47 story, according to the COMETA report, is that the evidence includes a microwave signal that seemed to originate from the object itself, giving away a position that corresponds to both the visual sighting and the radar track. This strange microwave signal turns up in other encounter incidents cited in the COMETA report, especially in cases where the instrumentation of chase aircraft seemed to have been shut down by the UFOs they were pursuing.

This is what seems to have happened in another eerily compelling incident in 1976 in the skies over Tehran just before the coup that overthrew the Shah. Here, an encounter with a UFO that dispatched a strange brilliantly lit object that scanned the interior of an Iranian F-4 Phantom jet also seems to defy conventional reality.

The incident began with a ground sighting, confirmed independently by other observers, that resulted in the vectoring of aircraft to the area to see if they could make visual contact with the mysterious object. In this case, the object was observed from the Tehran airport. Officials there contacted the military authorities, who in

272 □ William J. Birnes and Harold Burt

turn scrambled an American-made F-4 to close with the object. Upon its approach to the object, however, the F-4's instruments, including its radio, seemed to shut down, forcing the pilot to reverse his direction. At that point his instruments came back on-line.

A second F-4 also tried to close, but the object maintained a constant distance between itself and the interceptor. As the object began to change color right before the pilot's eyes, it seemed to dispatch a smaller object, appearing at first to be either a drone or slow-moving missile, toward the pursuing aircraft. When the pilot tried to lock on and fire a Sidewinder air-to-air missile at the object approaching him, he found that his fire control was inoperable, as well as his radio and intercom. With a strange object heading toward him and not knowing whether it was a weapon or something else, the pilot began a series of evasive maneuvers, climbing and diving as he tried in vain to escape the fast-approaching light. Finally the strange light reached the plane and passed right through the aircraft's interior before moving off and redocking with the large UFO, which then climbed out of sight. Had the Iranian Phantom jet just been scanned by an alien spaceship's remote sensing device?

COMETA placed a high credibility on this report, not only because of the confirmations on military radar as well as visual contacts, but because under combat conditions an F-4 on an intercept mission tried, but failed, to launch a missile at the object. Further, the report doubted that this could have been a natural occurrence because of the extremely high maneuverability of the strange light. The light had to have been controlled by some remote source to have been able to have overtaken the Phantom jet despite its high-speed evasive maneuvers.

In two final aerial encounter descriptions, the report cites an attempt at an interception with a UFO by Soviet fighter planes over Moscow, and an encounter with a brilliant object by an Argentine Airlines 727 that interfered with its landing at a local airport to the point that the electromagnetic effects of the object extinguished the street lights of the city and the runway lights at the airport. As in previous instances, the Argentine Airlines sighting was confirmed by multiple observers, lasted for more than one or two minutes, and produced ancillary electromagnetic effects. In the Moscow sighting, a report made by a Soviet Air Force general was carried in one of the national workers' newspapers in which he described the tight turns and maneuvers of a flying disk that was categorized as an aircraft of unknown origin.

The next section contained testimonies of sightings of flying saucers witnessed either on or near the ground by observers. There are stories of close encounters with flying saucers in France and a particularly interesting sighting of a UFO at close range by witnesses at a Russian missile site in 1989, just at the beginning of the devolution of the USSR into Russia and its federated republics. The case, declassified by the KGB in 1991, cited depositions given by military officers at the missile base in which they described their firsthand observations under conditions of good visibility, albeit shortly before midnight. In the sightings, up to three objects simultaneously were seen by military personnel over the missile base as they silently hovered overhead and then made rapid darting movements across the sky. When Russian chase planes appeared, the object rapidly accelerated and escaped the closing interceptors. It gave the impression to the observers as having originated from "another place," which, in their minds, perhaps meant "not of this world."

The Present State of Knowledge Concerning UFOs

In the second part of the report, COMETA discusses the ways investigations are conducted, how information is organized, and what we know about the results of these investigations, both past and present. It begins with a description of a plan to organize UFO research in France with the creation of a group to study unidentified aerospace phenomena. The group that was created was initially called GEPAN, for *Le Groupe d'études des phénomènes aérospatiaux non identifiés*. Its mission was to collect the thousands of reports from different organizations, including the police, and military and civilian aviation authorities. With a large array of official research and photo analysis at its disposal, GEPAN, and a later organization called SERPA, organized to study space objects that reentered Earth's atmosphere, and the French developed a formal plan to study UFOs. The plan called for an organization of all the reports into witnesses whose experiences could be taken as hard physiological or psychological evidence; the testimony of witnesses and their answers and reactions to specific questions about the event; physical pieces of evidence such as photographs or radar tapes; physical traces left on the ground such as residue or impressions left in grass or on crops; and finally the evidence of the psychological and social impact on people, including media reports.

After the initial study, each case in the records was classified into one of four categories:

A. A perfectly and clearly identified phenomenon.
B. A probably identifiable phenomenon that would be clear except for a few missing concrete elements.
C. A phenomenon that can't be identified because of a lack of facts necessary to make a determination.
D. A phenomenon that can't be identified despite an abundance of clear credible facts and data. In this case, the event defies categorization as a known event because the facts present don't correlate into something that's understandable in terms of natural occurrences.

After categorizing the outstanding cases presented in the report from French and foreign sources, the report writers focused on the study of category D, paying special attention to cases with high witness credibility. This includes such historic cases as the appearance of a strange craft at Socorro, New Mexico, which was similar to a UFO landing case in Trans-en-Provence on January 8, 1981. In this case, a circular object appeared in front of a witness standing in his garden, descended out of the sky, made a hard landing on a piece of flat ground near the witness's house, and then took off and disappeared into the sky. Similarities between this and other heavily documented cases led the report writers to conclude that there are some events where people have witnessed certain unidentifiable flying objects that display not only an exceptional aeronautical performance, but seem guided by a clear type of intelligence. The conclusion: some types of strange, intelligently guided, superior and advanced aircraft have visited Earth. And these conclusions come, not from a fringe group of true believers, but from a group of scientists, researchers, and former top-ranking military personnel.

In the subsequent chapter, the report tries to model the types of technology that might explain the ultra high maneuverability of UFOs, the silent and high-speed propulsion system, the ability of the UFOs to interfere with electronic devices, and the strange paralysis that UFOs sometimes seem to inflict upon witnesses. Studies into these levels of technology, the report reveals, are under way not only in France, but in other countries around the world. If the inspiration for these studies is merely a desire to advance to the next level of technology, there is nothing remarkable about this. However, if these studies are the result of UFO encounters around the world, then it means that new technologies are being inspired by our interaction with extraterrestrial intelligence.

The most promising type of experimentation with nonconventional propulsion systems is electromagnetic wave propagation. In these experiments, a powerful current is passed through electrodes so as to propagate a magnetic field. The displacement and reshaping of this field generates thrust. Although magnetic wave generation has been the subject of some experimentation, particularly in the United States, since the 1920s, there has been a rejuvenated interest in the technology. The United States has been particularly successful in experimenting with electromagnetic wave propagation in water, possibly for marine propulsion systems. Experiments in the air have been less successful, perhaps because new developments in the technology of superconductors still need to be realized before electromagnetic wave propagation in the atmosphere yields any real success.

Other possible methods of propulsion, according to the COMETA report, include antigravity devices, the harnessing of energy from imploding planets and stars, and—probably the closest to a conventional energy source—particle beam or directed energy devices. The report writers conclude that there is a perfectly reasonable model to account for the maneuvers of flying saucers or other unidentified flying objects.

How to account for the disturbance of electrical instruments is another matter that the report writers addressed. This intriguing issue was reported by a number of witnesses. Moreover, why did the interference of electrical instruments and motors seem so selective? The report suggests that some sort of microwave generating device interfered with the electrical flow so as to shut down radars, aircraft instruments, car motors, and perhaps even the Sidewinder missile launchers in the Iranian Phantom jets over Tehran. In the RB-47 incident over the southern United States, the unidentified object was detected by a microwave signal that seemed to be originating from inside it. A directed microwave signal is a variety of nonlethal weapon that's in use now, employed by the U.S. forces over Iraq during the Gulf War, and one of the variety of weapons that can shut down enemy communications under battlefield conditions. (Certain types of directed and concentrated electrical beam weapons are also being marketed to police departments in the United States to help them avoid wild and dangerous car chases by aiming the beam of electrons at the fugitive car so as to shut down its ignition system temporarily, allowing the police pursuit to catch up.) In this respect, the model that the COMETA report suggests is not only perfectly reasonable, it's already part of our own weapons array on Earth.

Similarly, the COMETA report suggested that the selective paralysis of some of the witnesses—which restricted the movement of their voluntary muscles without affecting their heart or breathing—might be the result of microwave bombardment. This is also borne out by weapons development here on Earth. The report points to experiments at the Advanced Air Force Weapons Laboratory at Kirtland Air Force Base in microwave weapons. However, the report doesn't mention the advanced Soviet development of microwave weapons which they deployed on the battlefield in Afghanistan and against NATO and U.S. helicopters and planes on maneuvers during the cold war. The French also experimented with wave-based weapons in the late 1960s and developed a device called "Jericho Trumpet," designed to shatter concrete walls through the intense focus of high-frequency sound waves.

What's interesting here is that the COMETA report assumes that whoever is piloting UFOs is deploying technology not so far ahead of our own that we cannot understand it. COMETA's models for what kinds of science may drive UFOs are consistent with our over-the-horizon development curve and may lead us to believe that the aliens, if in fact they are aliens, are not light-years beyond our capabilities. As for the microwave technology, if, in fact, the Soviets as well as the Americans have been experimenting with microwave weapons since the 1950s, and if one could assume, just for argument's sake, that some of the UFOs were experimental aircraft carrying certain nonlethal weapons, maybe a portion of the sightings involved rival military powers testing their aircraft against one another's defenses.

The Real Unknowns

When the panel members put all of the encounter stories, models, theories, and assessments together, the report concludes, in this second section, that a significant number of cases either demand further study or have to be classified "unknown." There's more than a fair share of balloon sightings, satellites burning up upon reentry to the atmosphere, and perhaps even bright stars that confused witnesses. There are also deliberate hoaxes, the report writers conclude, but these are actually a lot more rare than the debunkers would have people believe. However, there are enough "unknowns" to merit a separate category. The report now turns to the analysis of this category.

The report sets aside issues such as delusional behavior on the part of witnesses, mass hallucinations, mind control perpetrated upon citizens by secret agencies on both sides of the former Iron Curtain, deliberate disinformation campaigns to mask real government secrets, and secret government weapons programs that evolved during the cold war. Yet the report concedes that science must contend with the real possibility of ongoing extraterrestrial contact. It suggests that a large number of people already believe that UFOs are intelligently guided spaceships that have come from long distances across the universe and are probably surveilling our planet and making selective contact with human beings.

However, because of the vast distances that have to be covered in outer space, most scientists believe that the first contact, if it comes, between our species and a race of extraterrestrials will be through some kind of radio message. It might even be reported initially by SETI, the radio telescope array searching for signals of extraterrestrial life in the universe.

The COMETA report suggests that other scientists have developed another theory of interplanetary travel, a theory based on something called "space islands," either superhuge planetoid-size artificial structures or inhabitable asteroids that serve as spaceships with the travelers living in an interior environment. With an advanced propulsion system, even one based on a controlled matter-antimatter reaction within a containment field, these space islands could carry colonies of space settlers vast distances and launch ships that might be perceived as UFOs. Maybe just such a race of travelers has arrived in our solar system and has been making contact with us for the past fifty years or more.

At the end of its second section, the COMETA report evaluates UFO research in the United States, the United Kingdom, and Russia. It opens up an interesting window on American UFO research and demonstrates that, despite official denials of the reality of the existence of UFOs, unidentified flying objects have been continually studied at the highest levels of the Pentagon as a potential real threat to military security in the United States. While the U.S. government has engaged in a program of official denial, the report shows, a majority of Americans, according to recent surveys, believe that UFOs are real. At least 25 percent of all Americans believe that an extraterrestrial spaceship crashed outside of Roswell in 1947.

UFOs, the report reveals, have been spotted surveilling nuclear installations as well as military bases in the United States. The intelligence communities, both military and civilian, have studied the UFO problem and tried to ascertain the missions and intentions of these craft. These studies, the report says, have been augmented by many private studies and reports from academic and scientific associations. In particular, the report cites the Condon Report as an example of the disconnect between official U.S. policy and scientific analysis and evaluation.

Professor Edward Condon, project director of the University of Colorado study, wrote a deeply critical summary of the UFO issue as a preface to the Colorado Report, which had been commissioned by the U.S. Air Force. Yet the report itself suggested that UFOs posed significant scientific questions that demanded further study by the academic community. Rather than dismiss UFOs, the Colorado Report recommended that reported

UFO sightings and events should be evaluated and pursued as far as science allows. Yet the Condon executive summary, which (according to rumor) was encouraged by the air force, who wanted to extricate itself from the public UFO reporting business, almost completely dismissed the recommendations of its own attached report. Condon's summary did the job it was put up to do by allowing the U.S. Air Force to bow out of Project Blue Book once and for all.

The COMETA report next mentions Colonel Philip Corso's *The Day After Roswell* as another source of information regarding the U.S. government's policy toward UFOs. If, the COMETA report suggests, Corso's statements are even partially true, then the U.S. government has not only known about the existence of UFOs since 1947, but has undertaken a comprehensive development program to harvest the technology retrieved from downed UFOs into weapons systems and advanced technologies. These reverse-engineered technologies, such as super-tenacity fibers, lasers, fiber optics, microcircuitry, and night vision, although many of them were already in development before army R&D slipped them covertly to U.S. defense contractors, not only reveal that the United States has derived benefit from the military's encounter with UFOs, but also provides a basis in fact for the necessity of denial of UFOs.

What Colonel Corso's story suggests—although this is beyond the scope of the COMETA report—is that the United States Army is deliberately covering up its harvesting of alien technology by siphoning it into the military-industrial complex. It has a real economic stake in maintaining its denial of UFOs and the reverse-engineering program. That official denial was an integral part of army R&D director Lieutenant General Trudeau's strategy, even as early as 1958, to get the United States Congress to fund the reverse-engineering of extraterrestrial technology into advanced military weaponry. This was part of the reason, Colonel Corso revealed before he died in 1998, that the army required that all industrial developers of material from the R&D "Roswell drawer" own the patents on the technology they developed and even reverse-engineer the development reports. It would be the perfect cover and the foundation for denial that the technology—in General Trudeau's own words—was "not invented here."

The COMETA report also briefly documents information on UFO research in the United Kingdom, particularly its cooperation with the United States on various secret studies, and points to the discrepancy between UFO reports that have been made public and the continued official denial of the existence of UFOs. In summary fashion, the report covers UFO research in the former Soviet Union that has been released since the inception of Glasnost. It reveals more than one instance of unidentified objects surveilling Soviet missile and military installations. In one encounter, as cited earlier in the report, a Soviet fighter gave chase and the object simply moved out of the way as if the supersonic fighter were standing still.

Part of the problem in assessing the organization of UFO research in Russia is that many of the UFO events occurred during the cold war and fell under the provenance of the KGB. To this day researchers do not know the full extent of the KGB material still held as classified. Even more important, researchers don't know how much of the KGB's UFO file is composed of disinformation, part of the massive propaganda machine used as an information weapon during the cold war. Bit by bit, however, records of UFO encounters are coming to light, as scientists uncover records of crashes in remote areas of the former Soviet Union and interview witnesses who were present at the time. We don't know whether these craft were actual extraterrestrial spacecraft, unmanned U.S. surveillance aircraft, or downed U-2s, because Soviet military forces sealed off the sites to keep potential witnesses away.

UFOs and Defense

The final section of the COMETA report deals with the implications of UFO encounters for national and planetary defense. It also discusses the philosophical and social consequences of visitations by intelligent beings from other planets. The report asks what strategies human beings and their governments should develop not just to study UFOs, but—even assuming that only a small portion of the UFO sightings might be extraterrestrial craft—to figure out what their intentions might be. Why are they here? What are they looking for? And should we be looking for ways to establish contact with them?

How can we determine what the motivations might be of possible extraterrestrials, the report demands rather than asks. Should we look at them as potential threats or benevolent allies who are committed to our survival as a species? The writers suggest that researchers should be able to deduce something about the intentions of alien visitors from their behavior and the kinds of encounters they initiate, just as detectives can sometimes interpret the motives of a suspect from his behavior at a crime scene.

The presence of alien spacecraft over military installations and nuclear facilities could indicate a hostile intention. Why would they be surveilling our military facilities, probing defenses, and even provoking encounters with our aircraft if they weren't gathering technological intelligence or simply testing our ability to respond?

A more benign interpretation suggests that at least one purpose of alien incursions might be to protect us from either a deliberate or accidental nuclear holocaust that could destroy human civilization. Given the number of near accidents, including a recent incident in which Boris Yeltsin's military adviser went to the "suitcase" to initiate a prelaunch command code, a nuclear mistake is well within the range of possibility. And as nuclear weapons proliferate and the delivery systems emerging nuclear powers deploy to threaten their neighbors become more advanced than the management systems in place to control them, the chances of a nuclear mistake are on the increase. Perhaps these strange craft, the COMETA report suggests, are monitoring not our ability to defend ourselves from them, but our capacity for self-annihilation by releasing weapons of mass destruction that can set into motion their own chain of irreversible environmental events. That, and only that, might be the trigger for direct alien intervention in our planetary affairs.

But there's a third view, the report suggests. Alien contact has already been made with government agencies, and, under the cloak of deep secrecy, there is an ongoing transfer of technology. The report points specifically to the United States government, which after the incident at Roswell in 1947 seems to have developed an attitude of increasing secrecy. Was this as a result of a discovery of the vast potential of alien technology that suddenly fell into its power, as Colonel Corso said in *The Day After Roswell*?

Perhaps, the report suggests, it was to protect the knowledge of this new technology that motivated the United States military to shroud its study of UFOs in deep secrecy. The report points to the Nathan Twining "flying saucer" memo, whose existence was hidden for twenty-two years. It was revealed in the Condon Report that the United States had a policy to study the potential of flying saucers and the technology they possessed.

Other countries besides the United States and its NATO allies have been secretive about their possible UFO contacts, especially the Soviet Union. One has to wonder, therefore, whether there is a worldwide military conspiracy to cover up information about UFOs because no one wants to reveal what he may know and, in so doing, compromise military secrets gleaned from the retrieval of UFO contacts and accidental crashes. This military secrecy, the report suggests, spills over into governments as a whole and creates a climate of political secrecy. Is the entire human race being deprived of information about extraterrestrial cultures that might ultimately be beneficial?

The COMETA report, specifically addressing the UFO movement inside France, suggests that a superscientific organization become the repository of UFO investigative research. With the authority to catalog UFO-related information from official as well as nonofficial sources, which would enable it to develop working theories about UFOs, the organization would be able to answer questions about UFO encounters that cannot at present be answered because the information is too scattered among too many agencies, some of them top secret.

If a high-priority French agency works as a repository of research and decision making, then why not an all-European agency? the report writers ask. The study of UFOs and their intentions holds as much importance for all of Europe, including the UK, as it does for the French. The report suggests that European countries not only pool their knowledge and resources for the study of UFOs, but they become a kind of international lobby to encourage the United States to divulge its UFO secrets to them and ultimately to the rest of the world. The framework for such an international collaboration on the study of UFOs might well be the very same strategic alliances, such as NATO, that currently bind the Western military and economic powers. Such an organization devoted to the study of UFOs would be an unprecedented human endeavor to prepare all of us for the critical situations we may encounter should extraterrestrial contact become an open, public event.

Preparing for Contact

One of the primary questions the report asks is, What situations ought we to prepare ourselves for? What strategies must we develop should extraterrestrials make contact with us?

The report looks at the following scenarios:

1. A UFO appears, and its extraterrestrial passengers or flight crew express a desire to establish a public and peaceful contact with Earth's official representatives.
2. The accidental or deliberate discovery of an alien base either in France or somewhere else in Europe where the aliens may or may not have established a friendly presence.
3. A general invasion by extraterrestrials or a local attack at some strategic location.
4. A manipulation or disinformation campaign aimed at destabilizing national governments.

Perhaps this final strategy has already begun and both the secrecy and proliferation of reports are the substance of a campaign designed to weaken governments while preparing Earth's population for an alien presence. Perhaps that presence has already been established and the aliens themselves or their confederates on Earth are manipulating a vast public information and media campaign. If that's the case, who's left to determine what's true and what's false?

What strategies do we have to address each of the scenarios of alien contact that the COMETA report sets forth? If, as the report writers suggest, the ET hypothesis is "quasi-certain" because it is the only one that amalgamates all of the anecdotal and physical data into a cohesive explanation, then governments should openly work to develop strategies for contact. Openly critical of the United States for being ultrasecretive about UFO contacts, the report repeatedly stresses in its final section that European governments should urge the U.S. government to cooperate with its allies by sharing its information and to develop "contact" strategies should an emergency regarding UFO visitation arise.

While supporting its argument for an extraterrestrial hypothesis created from actual case histories, the credibility of the report also depends heavily on the credibility of its authors, who are not only members of the French scientific community, but military advisers as well. However, even while calling for greater cooperation among the world's powers to address the contingencies and strategies in planning for UFO contact, the report seems not to consider the obvious: that the primary reason for secrecy is that these contingency plans have already been drawn up or have been in existence for many years and governments don't want to share them with the general public. Perhaps it's true that individuals at the highest levels of government have either been aware of an extraterrestrial presence for years. Or, maybe at these levels government officials have actually been dealing with extraterrestrials and have reached a common accord with the extraterrestrials and among themselves that this knowledge should be kept secret until humanity can be prepared for some form of ultimate contact. This might very well be the reason that governments seem so oblivious to what the report writers see as clear and convincing evidence that UFO encounters have taken place.

Or maybe, some critics of the report have suggested, there's still another hypothesis. Maybe this report is itself a form of disinformation, or, better, disingenuous information, that's paving an intellectual path for disclosure. By laying the groundwork for conservative scientists to embrace a radical theory of ET contact, a contact that's already an ongoing process in the United States and other countries, maybe the COMETA report itself is part of the penultimate stage of disclosure. This is also something ufologists have to consider as they weigh the unsolved mysteries this report aims to resolve.

ABOUT THE AUTHORS

HAROLD BURT, the author of *Flying Saucers 101* (UFO Publishing, 2000), is a field investigator for MUFON International and a member of the board of directors for Orange County MUFON. When he is not investigating and writing about UFOs, Harold Burt manages his own Internet Web site company and is a sales manager for a major pharmaceutical company. Harold and his wife, Gina Burt, live in Dana Point, California, close enough to their grandchild to see him almost every day.

WILLIAM J. BIRNES, Ph.D., publisher of *UFO Magazine*, is the *New York Times* best-selling co-author of *The Day After Roswell* with Lt. Col. Philip J. Corso (Pocket, 1997). He has also co-authored *The Star Trek Cookbook,* with Ethan Phillips (Pocket, 1999); *Riverman* and *Signature Killers,* with Robert Keppel (Pocket, 1995 and 1997, respectively); *Serial Killers,* with Joel Norris (Doubleday, 1989), and was the editor-in-chief of the *McGraw-Hill Personal Computer Programming Encyclopedia* (McGraw-Hill, 1985; 2nd edition, 1989). William Birnes lives in Los Angeles with his wife, novelist, publisher, and Shadow Lawn Press partner Nancy Hayfield Birnes.

VISIT WARNER ASPECT ONLINE!

THE WARNER ASPECT HOMEPAGE
You'll find us at: www.twbookmark.com then by clicking on Science Fiction and Fantasy.

NEW AND UPCOMING TITLES
Each month we feature our new titles and reader favorites.

AUTHOR INFO
Author bios, bibliographies and links to personal websites.

CONTESTS AND OTHER FUN STUFF
Advance galley giveaways, autographed copies, and more.

THE ASPECT BUZZ
What's new, hot and upcoming from Warner Aspect: awards news, bestsellers, movie tie-in information . . .